MW01658525

Opening the Wisdom Door of the Madhyamaka School

by

Khenchen Palden Sherab Rinpoche

and

Khenpo Tsewang Dongyal Rinpoche

OPENING THE WISDOM DOOR OF THE
Madhyamaka School

by

Khenchen Palden Sherab Rinpoche

and

Khenpo Tsewang Dongyal Rinpoche

Edited by Andrew Cook *and* David Mellins

Opening the Wisdom Door of the Madhyamaka School

Published by Dharma Samudra.

Padma Samye Ling
618 Buddha Highway
Sidney Center, NY 13839
(607) 865-8068
www.padmasambhava.org

ISBN: 0-9659339-6-2

Contents

Acknowledgements

The Samye Translation Group would like to thank everyone who was involved in helping bring this project to fruition. In particular, we would like to thank Andrew Cook for his joyful and diligent efforts in completing this book and editing these transcriptions. Without his aspirations and hard work, this book could not have been completed in such a short period of time. Thanks are also well deserved by David Mellins and Keith Endo for their extensive help with editing, and by Ann Helm for her help with the Tibetan and Sanskrit terms. We would also like to thank the many people who helped transcribe these teachings, including Ani Joanie Andras, Mary Ann Doychak, Keith Endo, Beba Febo, Colin Foote, and Pema Tara. Additional thanks goes out to Rita Frizzell for her assistance in preparing the text and cover for publishing, to Sujata Ghosh for her help with final editing, and to Pema Dragpa for his work with editing and layout.

As always, we are deeply grateful to Ani Lorraine O'Rourke and Pema Tsultrim for their steadfast administrative help with Padmasambhava Buddhist Center.

We would also like to thank all the resident staff of Padma Samye Ling whose work actively supports the Khenpo Rinpoches' activities locally and internationally. We also wish to extend our thanks to all members and friends of the Padmasambhava Buddhist Center worldwide for their constant support over many years.

Most importantly, we offer our heartfelt gratitude and devotion to the Venerable Khenpo Rinpoches for blessing us with the opportunity to receive and practice these profound teachings. We humbly request that Khenchen Palden Sherab Rinpoche and Khenpo Tsewang Dongyal Rinpoche continue to turn the wheel of Dharma, and we offer prayers for their long and healthy lives.

We sincerely ask forgiveness from all wisdom beings, holders of the teachings, and readers for all errors and misinterpretations of the teachings present in this text. We welcome any suggestions on how to improve the text.

May everyone who reads this book understand the value and meaning of their precious human life. May their highest aspirations be fulfilled for the benefit of all beings.

Shedra Year Three: Svatantrika Madhyamaka

Teaching:	The Svatantrika Madhyamaka of Shantarakshita (Yogachara Svatantrika Madhyamaka) according to the commentaries of Mipham Rinpoche and Longchenpa.
Teachers:	Venerable Khenchen Palden Sherab Rinpoche and Venerable Khenpo Tsewang Dongyal Rinpoche.
Time:	August 27 to September 1, 2005.
Place:	Palden Padma Samye Ling Monastery and Retreat Center, Upstate New York.
Retinue:	Thirty to forty students came from around the world to participate in six days of intensive study of Tibetan Buddhist philosophy.

Introduction

We should begin by restrengthening our beautiful bodhichitta motivation by thinking of all living beings, who extend as far as space. Keep the following intention in your mind: "In order to liberate all sentient beings into the state of perfect enlightenment, I am going to listen to, contemplate, and practice the profound and essential teachings of Buddha Shakyamuni known as Madhyamaka."

Over the past two years, we have had the wonderful opportunity to briefly discuss some of the philosophical systems of Buddhism, according to our time and capabilities. Everything we practice is based on this philosophy. But what does it really mean to study Buddhist philosophy? It means we are engaging in and understanding the profound meaning of the true nature exactly as it is, by discovering the truth without any exaggeration or depreciation. It is therefore very important to have a correct philosophical view. The Madhyamaka teachings are as profound and deep as an ocean. And in this shedra we will try to enter the depths of the ocean of Madhyamaka, rather than hang out on Madhyamaka's beach! So let us try and deepen ourselves by taking a dip in the vast ocean of Madhyamaka.

There are two different schools of Madhyamaka: *Svatantrika* Madhyamaka, or *Rangyupa* [*rang rgyud pa*], and *Prasangika* Madhyamaka, or *Thalgyurpa* [*thal 'gyur pa*].[1] These two schools present profound and sophisticated philosophical systems, both within the specific context of Buddhism and in the more general context of human history. Before going a bit deeper into the Svatantrika Madhyamaka school, we will give an overview of the wider span of Madhyamaka teachings. It is important to understand Prasangika *and* Svatantrika Madhyamaka, since each school is very profound; however, we don't have enough time to cover both in detail, and simply reviewing them might not be very beneficial. So we have decided that during this shedra we will mainly focus on Svatantrika Madhyamaka.

The Madhyamaka philosophy is a teaching of Buddha Shakyamuni, who began his spiritual journey by developing the thought of enlightenment known as "bodhichitta." After cultivating bodhichitta, he continually accumulated the two merits for three countless aeons.[2] Finally, the Blessed One reached complete enlightenment—the state of buddhahood. He then began to share the knowledge and wisdom he gained through his practice and meditation Mipham Rinpoche[3] praises the sublime achievement of the Buddha: "You achieved the ultimate state of realization and discovered the nectar of the Dharma. Filled with love and compassion, you shared this nectar with living beings without any trace of self-importance or ego-clinging." This nectar is the authentic message of the Buddha, based upon his realization of the truth. He shared this realization with beings to lead them to liberation. What we are experiencing now is the glorious nectar of the Dharma, and we will drink it according to our capabilities.

The Buddha taught about the truth of the nature as it is. He did not describe the nature to be fancier than it is, nor did he attempt to inspire or please others by exaggerating. In the same way, the Supreme Teacher did not subtract anything from the truth in order to avoid displeasing others. He taught the truth in a straightforward manner, exactly as it is. Truth is truth. But in order to help small, dualistic minds understand the nature, the Blessed One taught the Dharma according to different levels of subtlety, with each level corresponding to unique dualistic fixations and the various ways the nature is perceived by various types of mind. These teachings are known as the 84,000 teachings of the Buddha. Yet Buddha Shakyamuni was not randomly trying to show us different things: Again, he taught according to the readiness of our dualistic minds so that we could understand in terms of our capacity, accept the validity of the teachings, and develop progressively greater understanding.

The 84,000 Teachings of the Buddha

All the teachings of the buddha are encompassed by three seminal teachings known as the three "turnings of the wheel of Dharma." A great Dzogchen tantra states that the Buddha gave different teachings in order to subdue the three poisons of anger, attachment, and ignorance. To dispel the attachment of sentient beings, Buddha gave 21,000 teachings on the Vinaya. To dispel anger, Buddha gave 21,000 teachings on the Sutras. To dispel ignorance, Buddha gave 21,000 teachings on the Abhidharma. Finally, so that all three poisons could be dispelled and subdued, Buddha gave 21,000 teachings on the Tantras.

These teachings do not essentially contradict one another because all of us are afflicted by the three poisons of attachment, anger, and ignorance, and these poisons need to be uprooted and removed. For this reason, any Dharma teaching we apply is always good, since it will directly remove the obstacles and obscurations that prevent joy and realization; all Dharma teachings are extremely special. The 84,000 teachings are alternately divided into three or nine yanas, or "vehicles," according to the various ways we can classify the teachings.[4] In any case, the yanas become deeper and more sophisticated as they progress; this is how the Buddha skillfully leads the childlike minds of individual sentient beings along the path to enlightenment. The teachings become deeper as we grow and our understanding becomes more subtle. Therefore, the teachings of the first yana are less sophisticated than the teachings of the second yana, and the second yana is less sophisticated than the third yana, etc. Each yana includes the teachings of the yanas that precede it, so the presentation of the nature as it is becomes more refined and accurate as one moves up the different vehicles. This trend continues through all nine yanas. In general, this is how the system of the nine yanas functions in terms of the minds of different sentient beings.

First, it is very important to understand the "view" and base our practice upon this understanding.[5] The view is our goal and target. Once we have established this view, we can progress along the path and eventually achieve our goals. Hence, the view is the foundation of both the path and its result, or fruition. In Tibetan Buddhism it is often said, "Madhyamaka is the view, Mahamudra is the path, and Dzogpa Chenpo is the result." Madhyamaka, Mahamudra, and Dzogchen are not contradictory or isolated from each other; they are all connected. So we follow a particular path according to our view, and, as we continue, we discover the view as it is.

Beginning Discussion of Madhyamaka

Madhyamaka is known as *Uma* [*dbu ma*] in Tibetan. *Uma* means "middle" or "center." It is this "middle view" or "middle way" we are going to uncover and explore through the techniques of Madhyamaka. But why is Madhyamaka referred to as the "Middle Way"? It is called the Middle Way because it is not extreme; Madhyamaka is not right wing or left wing. These are the ultimate teachings of the Buddha. In Tibetan Buddhist philosophy, this ultimate view is known as *ngedon* [*nges don*], literally "definitive truth." Ngedon refers to the certain, definitive, inevitable meaning of the nature as it is. Since there is nothing further to add and nothing to subtract from Madhyamaka, it is known as definitive. By directly referring to the nature as it is, Madhayamaka explains the ultimate meaning of truth, the nature of all things.

As we mentioned earlier, the Buddha gave three or four seminal teachings known as the turnings of the wheel of Dharma. Madhyamaka comes from the second and third turnings, and the Vajrayana teachings—sometimes known as the "fourth turning of the wheel of Dharma"—are based upon Madhyamaka. Consequently, Madhyamaka is the essence of the Buddha's second, third, and fourth seminal teachings. Generally speaking, Madhyamaka comes from the *Prajnaparamita* teachings of the second turning of the wheel of Dharma. *Prajnaparamita* means "transcendent wisdom" or "perfection of wisdom, and is the foundation of the third and fourth turnings as well. The philosophical system of the *Prajnaparamita* teachings was made popular by the great masters Nagarjuna and Asanga, who were predicted several times by Buddha Shakyamuni in different Mahayana sutras and tantras. Nagarjuna, the first Madhyamaka teacher, was born about four hundred years after the Blessed One's mahaparinirvana.

The Buddha's teachings on the *Prajnaparamita* are very sophisticated, very profound, and very vast, so they are difficult to immediately understand. But Nagarjuna summarized the philosophy of *Prajnaparamita* in a condensed way that is easy to follow. He wrote a very famous book called the *Mula-madhyamaka-karikas*, or *Mula-madhyamaka-prajna*. In Tibetan, this work is called *Uma tsa wa'i sherab*,and it is sometimes translated into English as the *Root Verses on Madhyamaka*.[6] The *Mula-madhyamaka-prajna* has twenty-seven chapters. Yet these chapters are not based on Nagarjuna's own presumptions—he was not just guessing. Instead, this work relies on logic, reason, and the reader's own intelligence to explore and introduce the nature as it is. The great Nagarjuna wrote four or five additional texts to further support and explain the root text of the *Mula-madhyamaka-prajna*. These are called the *Six Treastises of the Reasoning of Madhyamaka*. Altogether, these texts clearly establish the view of Madhyamaka.

Nagarjuna was the second head abbot of Nalanda Monastic University, and many great masters and scholars came to study at Nalanda during the time of its flourishing. Arya Nagarjuna had several great disciples, one of whom was Buddhapalita, a master renowned for his understanding of Madhyamaka philosophy. Buddhapalita wrote a very famous commentary on Nagarjuna's *Mula-madhyamaka-prajna* entitled *Buddhapalita-vrtti*, or *The Commentary of Buddhapalita*. Like all great Buddhist masters of his time, Buddhapalita was Indian, and he too was studying and teaching at Nalanda. In his commentary on *The Root Verses on Madhyamaka*, Buddhapalita directly establishes that everything is within the profound state of great emptiness. Again, this work was very popular in India and at Nalanda around the time it was written.

Bhavaviveka Refutes Buddhapalita

Between thirty and one hundred years later, another great master was born in southern India. His name was Acharya Bhavya, or

Bhavaviveka, also known as Lobpon Bhavya and Leg Den Je. Bhavaviveka had studied all the Madhyamaka texts, including Nagarjuna's *Mula-madhyamaka-prajna*, as well as Buddhapalita's commentary on this work. He refuted certain aspects of the *Buddhapalita-vrtti*, arguing that Buddhapalita had gone too far in establishing great emptiness. Of course, Bhavaviveka used solid reasoning to support his refutation. He claimed that Buddhapalita's commentary was not the correct way to present and explain great emptiness to other disciples and practitioners. Acharya Bhavya's famous commentary on the *Mula-madhyamaka-karikas* is called *Sherab Dronma*—the *Lamp of Wisdom*,[7] and it is in this text that he contradicts different parts of Buddhapalita's commentary. The *Lamp of Wisdom* outlines the principal philosophical system of Acharya Bhavya, explaining that we should understand relative truth according to the Sautrantika school of the Hinayana. From this perspective, on the relative level everything we see externally is formed by atoms. Furthermore, perception is inseparable from mind, but the objects we see perceive are made of matter. And this matter is composed of atoms. Therefore all the objects of the senses are compounded—made of atoms—and these objects are experienced through the perceptions and conceptions of mind. This is the level of relative truth.

In contrast, on the level of absolute truth everything is empty: All phenomena composed of atoms are empty, and all perceptions, conceptions, and states of consciousness are empty as well. Based upon this understanding of the absolute, it should be recognized that everything is totally empty. Bhavaviveka explains that we should maintain this understanding of emptiness on the absolute level, but on the relative level we should precisely follow the philosophical understanding of the Sautrantika school of the Hinayana. As we said, this interpretation of Madhyamaka from the *Lamp of Wisdom* became very popular, and is known as the Sautrantika Madhyamaka school, or the Sautrantika Svatantrika Madhyamaka school.

Bhavaviveka was truly a great master of Mahayana Buddhism. In addition to his *Lamp of Wisdom*, which is a word commentary on Nagarjuna's *Root Verses on Madhyamaka*, Acharya Bhavya wrote a *meaning* commentary on the same work entitled *Madhyamaka-hrdaya*, or *Umai nyingpoi tsig ler chepa.*[8] This is roughly translated into English as *Verses on the Essence of Madhyamaka*. He then wrote a third book—a commentary on his own *Verses on the Essence of Madhyamaka*—called *Madhyamaka-hrydaya-tarka-jvala*, the *Blaze of Reasoning*. These last two works are considered to be essence or meaning commentaries on Nagarjuna's works.

Chandrakirti Refutes Bhavaviveka

Several generations after Bhavaviveka, the great Indian master Chandrakirti was born. Eventually Chandrakirti also became the head abbot of Nalanda. He had studied the *Mula-madhyamaka-prajna* commentaries of both Buddhapalita and Acharya Bhavya, and believed that Buddhapalita's work was perfect. As a result, Chandrakirti refuted Bhavavikeka's teaching, which had since become the basis of the popular Svatantrika Madhyamaka school. He claimed that Bhavavivekas's teachings were more distracting than those of Buddhapalita, since they did not immediately lead to absolute truth. Therefore, he argued, Acharya Bhavya created many distracting conceptual layers and detours to practitioners' realization of the absolute. Chandrakirti reasoned that all the different systems and methods concerning matter, mass, and consciousness merely relate with relative truth, and relative truth is both deceiving and distracting. He questioned, "Why should we spend time worrying about relative truth when it distracts practitioners from the true nature? As Buddhapalita taught, we should immediately arrive at the absolute truth of emptiness. This method is accurate, true, and doesn't mix anything up."

The great master Chandrakirti wrote two very famous commentaries on Madhyamaka. First is the *Mula-madhyamaka-vrtti-*

prasannapada, or *Clear Words*, more commonly known as *Prasannapada*. This is called *Tsig Salwa* [*tshig gsal ba*] in Tibetan. Second is the *Madhyamakavatara*, or *Entrance to the Middle Way*. The *Prasannapada* is a commentary that explains the words of Nagarjuna's *Mula-madhyamaka-prajna*, whereas the *Madhyamakavatara*, or *Uma la jugpa* [*dbu ma la 'jug pa*], is a commentary on the meaning of Madhyamaka. These works created the foundation of the Prasangika Madhyamaka school of Buddhism; because Chandrakirti emphasized a direct approach to absolute truth, he is known as the second great Prasangika master. We might say that Buddhapalita was the first master of Prasangika Madhyamaka, but Chandrakirti became the most famous. Others argue that Chandrakirti himself was actually the founder of the Prasangika Madhyamaka school.

Shantarakshita and Madhyamaka

The great Indian master Shantarakshita was born shortly after, or even during, the time of Chandrakirti.[9] Like Chandrakirti before him, Shantarakshita eventually became the head abbot of Nalanda Monastic University. He was also the principal teacher of the king of Bengal, and, as you all know, the cofounder of Tibetan Buddhism. Shantarakshita studied all the Madhyamaka texts we have been discussing, and he wrote his own commentary on the *Mula-madhyamaka-prajna* of Nagarjuna known as the *Madhyamakalankara*, or the *Ornament of Madhyamaka*. He then wrote another text known as *Madhyamakalankara-svavrtti*, otherwise known as the *Auto Commentary on the Madhyamakalankara*.[10]

The great master Shantarakshita explained relative truth according to the Mind Only philosophical school [*Sems tsam pa*]. This school regards all relative phenomena as mind: subject, object, and mind itself are all held to be mind. So, Shantarakshita describes *relative* truth in the tradition of the great masters Asanga and Vasubandhu, exactly according to the Mind Only view. In terms of *absolute* truth, however, he follows the teachings of Nagarjuna. Thus Shantarakshita combines the understanding of Mind Only and Madhyamaka into a single philosophy by merging the teachings of Asanga/Vasubandhu and Nagarjuna into a single state. Normally these two schools are considered to be two major, independent schools of thought. For this reason, Shantarakshita's lineage teaching of this philosophical doctrine is known as Chittamatra Madhyamaka or Mind Only Madhyamaka. More precisely, it is known as Yogachara Svatantrika Madhyamaka.

Shantarakshita's teacher was Yeshe Nyingpo (Skt. Jnanagarbha), another famous Madhyamaka master who taught at Nalanda. Yeshe Nyingpo wrote a very popular book on Madhyamaka known as *Denpa nyi nampar chepa* [*bDen pa gnyis rnam par 'byed pa*; Skt. *Satya-dvaya-vibhanga*], the *Division of the Two Truths*. This text provided an explanation of Madhyamaka very similar to that of Shantarakshita's, except Yeshe Nyingpo did not specify that relative truth should be understood as described in the Mind Only school. Shantarakshita's most renowned disciple, Kamalashila, came to Tibet after he himself arrived in the Land of Snows. Kamalashila also wrote a famous book on Madhyamaka—consistent with Shantarakshita's presentation—known as *Uma nangwa* [*dBu ma snang ba*; Skt. *Madhyamakaloka*), the *Light on Madhyamaka*. This very famous text is not exactly a commentary, but rather a general work on the subject of Madhyamaka.

Jnanagarbha—the teacher of Shantarakshita—Shantarakshita himself, and Kamalashila are generally regarded as the most renowned masters of Svatantrika Madhyamaka. When we divide Madhyamaka into Prasangika and Svatantrika, they are always classified as belonging to the Svatantrika school. These masters are often referred to as the "three great masters of the east," since they all came from India, Bengal, and the surrounding area. Examining the history of India, we discover that Svatantrika Madhyamaka was very popular there, where it was taught by masters such as Bhavaviveka and the three great masters of the east.

Questions and Answers

Question: Could you say a little bit more about how Yogachara Madhyamaka developed based upon the Cittamatra, or Mind Only school?

Answer: I think you all know that *Yogachara* is a synonym for the Mind Only school, which is called *sem tsam pa* in Tibetan. The terms *Yogachara* and *Cittamatra* are both Sanskrit words. Roughly translated, *yoga* refers to an inner state of concentration and is deeply connected with the mind. *Chara* means "conduct" or "action." So *Yogachara* can be translated as "action of the mind." The Mind Only schools sees everything in the world and beyond as none other than the emanations and activities of mind. There are two ways to understand this. First, all schools agree that one's own perceptions, conceptions, and ideas are mind. These are associated with the perceiving subject. Next, we have to look at seemingly "objective" phenomena, such as mountains, the world, the galaxy, and other objects. What are these? You may wonder how these phenomenal objects could be projections of mind.

The Mind Only school teaches that our habits patterns of grasping to phenomena as substantially solid and inherently existent have been continually imprinted in the subconscious storehouse (Skt. *alaya*), or the eighth consciousness.[11] Based upon these imprints, our perceptual habit patterns reflect back to ourselves and others as phenomenal appearances. Although objects seem to be distinct from mind, they all begin with mind. Generally, we have accumulated habit patterns: (1) the habit pattern of (perceiving things) as singular and solid, which is the universal habit pattern; (2) the habit pattern of perceiving phenomenal appearances, which are the objects of the senses; and (3) the habit patterns of individual, physical characteristics. Even though these three habit patterns appear to be different from mind itself, they are actually imprints that have been stored in the alaya for a very long time. At the present time, these imprints (objects) are reflecting back to ourselves (subjects), despite the fact that they are manifestations of mind previously registered in the alaya. In this way, external objects and all phenomena are actually part of mind's own display; on the absolute level, nothing substantially solid has ever existed throughout beginningless time. phenomena are like illusions or magic. This is the principal philosophy of the Yogachara schools.

The great Shantarakshita incorporated this Mind Only view of conventional reality in the Yogachara Madhyamaka school, which therefore describes relative reality in precisely the same manner as the Mind Only school. On the absolute level, however, Madhyamaka describes everything as empty. Even mind itself it seen to be empty and devoid of inherent self-existence. Shantarakshita united these two profound philosophical systems—the Yogachara view of conventional reality and the Madhyamaka view of absolute truth—without any hardship or contradiction. To summarize, on the relative level, everything is a display of mind; on the absolute level, everything is completely beyond all characteristics and complexity.

In the *Madhyamakalankara*, Khenchen Bodhisattva himself describes the Yogachara Madhyamaka school as "riding the chariot of two great philosophical systems, holding the reins of logic and reasoning." And what are these two great chariots? They are the profound Madhyamaka system of Nagarjuna and the vast philosophical system of Asanga and Vasubandhu combined together in a single state of practice. Based upon this profound system of logic and reason—applied in meditation—we will proceed directly to the perfect state of buddhahood.

Question: You say that, since beginningless time, mind has created everything, even atoms. So mind created that wall right there...could you put this in an evolutionary context for us?

Answer: [Rinpoches laughing.] Yes, that is really true! If we look closely, we will see that this entire building was created by mind; mind projected the building, mind made the plans, mind carried out those plans, and mind constructed the building with different materials. And, as you pointed out, all atoms are also created by mind, or habitual patterns. Our habitual patterns developed a very long time ago. In fact, since beginningless time we have been busy creating and reinforcing habit patterns. For instance, the habit patterns of mind gave rise to the four elements: earth, fire, water, and wind.

One of the main habit pattern shared by sentient beings is the habit of solidity, the tendency to perceive things as solid. When this habit pattern of solidity is strongly developed, it appears as the earth element. The habit pattern of moisture or liquid appears as the water element. The habit pattern of warmth appears as the fire element. The habit pattern of movement appears as the wind element. So the four elements develop based upon our habit patterns, developing the physical body and phenomena. These habit patterns reflect outwardly in a variety of different ways as the objects of the five senses: form, sound, smell, taste, and touch (i.e. feeling). The habit pattern of spaciousness reflects externally as the sky. Each of these "external" reflections is based upon the habit patterns of the mind. This is why the Mind Only school and many Buddhist teachers explain that our environment and the whole universe begin in the mind, and are none other than mind's own reflections. Even though it seems to be the opposite—that everything begins outside—deep down, the reverse is actually true; everything starts inwardly and projects externally.

Our habitual patterns and karmic imprints are stored in the *alaya*, which is often translated as the "subconscious storehouse," the "all-base," or the "all-ground." In a way, all the karma we produce through volitional action[12] is stored in the alaya as a karmic imprint or habitual tendency. When corresponding causes and conditions come together, karmic tendencies begin to reflect externally as the waves and echoes of these imprints. We call this "karmic vision," "karmic experience," or "karmic activity."

Our meditation practice cleanses and purifies the karmic imprints on the alaya, and we begin to create new habit patterns associated with enlightenment. When we completely dissolve and remove the negative habit patterns of mind through our meditation on the great emptiness of the true nature, we are freed from the habit patterns of grasping to phenomena as substantially solid, and we achieve perfect enlightenment. Once more, as we purify the alaya, habit patterns of solidity begin to dissolve, and the space element becomes more predominant. When the habit patterns of wisdom become stronger and stronger, mundane habit patterns related with misperceiving the nature completely disappear, and we begin to perceive the external universe as a pureland and ourselves as an enlightened being, or deity. This is a brief explanation of why mind is the basis of everything.

History

How Svatantrika Madhyamaka Came to Tibet

But how did Shantarakshita's philosophical system come to Tibet? Of course you probably know that Khenchen Shantarakshita himself travelled to the Land of Snows. There he taught Svatantrika Madhyamaka, although he did not specifically use the word "Svatantrika" to describe his philosophy; it was simply part of the philosophical teachings he gave in Tibet during the 8th century.[13] The twenty-five disciples of Guru Padmasambhava and other great masters of that time were all schooled in the philosophical system rooted in the Svatantrika Madhyamaka school. That is, Svatantrika Madhyamaka was the *only* form of Madhyamaka taught in 8th century Tibet. Although both Svatantrika and Prasangika texts were translated during the time of Shantarakshita, it wasn't until the 11th century that Prasangika became more widespread and activated in the Land of Snows.

A great Tibetan master named Ngok Lotsawa Loden Sherab lived in Tibet during the 11th century. He was also a great translator and teacher. Loden Sherab was born in central Tibet, but he left the Land of Snows at the age of seventeen to travel to India, particularly to the area of Kashmir. He stayed in India for seventeen years before returning to the Tibet, at which time he began teaching in central Tibet. Lotsawa Loden Sherab became so renowned that each time he gave a teaching ten or even twenty thousand disciples would gather to listen. It is often said that there was no room large enough to hold all his disciples, so he would teach in a meadow or on the plain ground outside. It is also said that when he taught there were no obstacles: He would simply stand up on the throne facing east and *teach* the disciples in that direction, before turning to teach the disciples in the southern, western, and northern directions. The Tibetan histories recount that at the end of his teachings, everybody would say *lekpar song* [*legs par gsungs*], which is like the Sanskrit exclamation "sadhu!" It means "wonderful." So everybody would say "Wonderful! Wonderful!" This is still done today in Sri Lanka.

At this time in 8th century Tibet, they used a special book holder called a *shokala*. When the teachings concluded, everyone would close their books at the same time. The sound of these books shutting was so loud that it would echo throughout the mountains, startling horses and other animals. Loden Sherab's philosophical teachings are classified along with those of Acharya Bhavya and the three great masters of the east. Thus, he is also renowned as a Svatantrika Madhyamaka master in the tradition of Shantarakshita.

Loden Sherab eventually became the head of Sangphu Monastic University in central Tibet. According to Tibetan history, Samye was Tibet's first monastic university and Sangphu was its second. Many great masters of Tibetan Buddhism, including the Omniscient Longchenpa, started their education at Sangphu. Ngok Lotsawa Loden Sherab was the second abbot of this monastery and he was responsible for making Sangphu so famous. It was founded in the 11th century and survived through the late fifteenth or 16th century. Sangphu truly became one of the greatest centers of studying, learning, and knowledge in all of Tibet. Upon reading the histories, you will find that all the great masters of Tibetan Buddhism before the 16th century—regardless of their particular school—studied at Sangphu monastery. Briefly, Loden Sherab was a very famous master of Svatantrika Madhyamaka.

Lotsawa Loden Sherab had many renowned students, including Tolung Gyamarwa [*stod lung rgya dmar ba*] and Tolungwa [*gro lung* ba], who were very famous. Because these disciples were great adherents of the Svatantrika Madhyamaka school, they were also followers of the three great masters of the east and Bhavaviveka. Later on, another remarkable master appeared in Tibet named Chapa Chokyi Senge, who eventually became the head teacher of Sangphu monastery. He was a very famous logician and practitioner, regarded as an exceptional follower of the masters of the east and Acharya Bhavya. Chapa Chokyi Senge himself had many famous disciples, among whom the most renowned were known as the "eight line disciples of Chapa Chokyi Senge." Each one of these disciples became a very famous logician and scholar, following the Svatantrika Madhyamaka philosophical school. Generally speaking, the Madhyamaka philosophical system is based upon logic, philosophy, and correct view—all three are united together. Thus, each of these Svatantrika teachers was also an expert logician. Chapa Chokyi Senge is one of the greatest logicians in Tibetan history. In fact, in a way he is the founder of Tibet's system of debate. Although Buddhist debate already existed in India, the Tibetan debate system and style were invented by Chokyi Senge.

Around the same time as the eight line sons of Chapa, the glorious master Sakya Pandita appeared in Tibet. One of the greatest masters of Tibetan Buddhism, Sakya Pandita became the royal teacher of the youngest Tibetan prince. He was an accomplished master of Svatantrika Madhyamaka, a hence follower of the three great masters of the east and Acharya Bhavya.

When we speak of all these distinguished logicians and masters, we are not simply referring to intellectuals; these beings were also great practitioners who achieved the highest realization by practicing Madhyamaka in combination with the Vajrayana teachings. Both Svatantrika and Prasangika Madhyamaka were popular in India, but Svatantrika Madhyamaka was especially widespread. Many of the great Indian masters—such as the eighty-four mahasiddhas—followed the philosophy of the Svatantrika Madhyamaka school. As we explained earlier, this philosophy later came to Tibet and influenced the twenty five disciples of Guru Padmasambhava. Consequently, the philosophy of the twenty-five disciples is also based upon the Svatantrika Madhyamaka school. The same can be said for the eighty mahasiddhas of the Yerpa region.[14] All the students of Loden Sherab practiced according to the Svatantrika view, along with the skillful means of the Vajarayana, reaching the highest level of realization. This is just a brief history about how Svatantrika Madhyamaka was transmitted and became popular in India and Tibet, up until the eleventh or 12th century.

How Prasangika Madhyamaka Came to Tibet

While Prasangika Madhyamaka is often referred to as the philosophical teachings of Chandrakirti, it actually includes the teachings of both Chandrakirti and Buddhapalita. Prasangika Madhyamaka was also translated into Tibetan during the 8th century, the time of Guru Padmasambhava and Shantarakshita, but it was never as popular as Svatantrika Madhyamaka. In terms of ultimate meaning, Svatantrika Madhyamaka and Prasangika Madhyamaka agree: For both schools, the absolute meaning is the same, so there they are not so different in that respect. It is only the method through which each school establishes the ultimate philosophical view that differs. Again, Prasangikas and Svatantrikas agree on the essential nature of absolute truth.

After the time of Lotsawa Loden Sherab—sometime at the end of the eleventh or the beginning of the 12th century—another noble being appeared in Tibet whose name was Patsap Nyima Dragpa. Nyima Dragpa also travelled to northwest India to study in the pocket of Buddhist activity in Kashmir, eventually becoming a great translator and master before returning to Tibet. Nyima Dragpa became interested in Prasangika Madhyamaka and devoted himself to this philosophical system. He corrected and retranslated Chadrakirti's *Prasannapada*, or *Tsig Tsel* (*Clear Words*), teaching Prasangika Madhyamaka to his disciples using the *Madhyamakavatara*. As a result, the Prasangika tradition grew in popularity during this period in Tibet.

When Nyima Dragpa initially began teaching Prasangika Madhyamaka in Tibet he did not have many followers. Thereafter, however, another great Kadampa master began sending his disciples to study with the famed Sharawa, who specifically taught Chandrakirti's

Madhyamakavatara. Due to the efforts of these students, many Tibetan practitioners soon became interested in the Prasangika Madhyamaka school. For this reason, there was a rapid growth of the Prasangika Madhyamaka school in Tibet during this period.

It was around this time that Chapa Chokyi Senge was said to have eight lines of spiritual sons, sometimes referred to as the "sons of the eight great lines." Among these spiritual sons was Magda Changchub. Because he was a disciple of Chapa Chokyi Senge, Magda studied Svatantrika Madhyamaka; nevertheless, he was also interested in the Prasangika philosophical system. Thus, Magda Changchub continued his studies of Prasangika Madhyamaka under Patsap Nyima Dragpa, eventually becoming one of the greatest Prasangika masters of Tibet. In later Tibetan histories, Patsap Nyima Dragpa is said to have four spiritual sons, or renowned disciples, including Magda Changchub. Hence, Magda Janchub is considered to be a spiritual son of both Chapa Chokyi Senge as well as Patsap Nyima Dragpa.

But what is the *real* difference between Svatantrika and Prasangika Madhyamaka? In essence, there are no big differences between these schools; the only significant distinction lies in the methods each tradition uses to establish the two truths, or relative truth and absolute truth. Regarding their presentations of the absolute level with respect to the principal "view," they are the same. So both schools are very similar, differing only in very subtle ways.

This has been a brief history of the two Madhyamaka schools, including how they originated in India and later arrived in Tibet. It is very beneficial to know the history of how these Madhyamaka schools began and gained popularity. After Sharawa's teaching on Prasangika Madhyamaka, this philosophical school became well-known and widely practiced in Tibet, and has remained so until the present. Along with Svatantrika Madhyamaka, Prasangika Madhyamaka is now a principal subject of meditation in all the schools of Tibetan Buddhism. The Dzogchen tantra known as *Ati kopa chenpai gyu* (*Ati bkod pa chen pa'i rgyud*) emphasizes the importance of understanding a given teaching's history, explaining that it is hard to have confidence in a teaching without exploring its history. This is said in various teachings. We have begun our shedra by following this tradition and mentioning the names of just a few of the great Madhyamaka masters of India and Tibet.

Among the Indian and Tibetan masters we just mentioned, a few contemplated and practiced Madhyamaka in combination with Dzogchen and tantra teachings, thus reaching high realization. Each of the eighty-four mahasiddhas—these wonderful Indian and Tibetan masters—were practitioners of Madhyamaka as well as Dzogchen. There have been countless practitioners and masters who achieved realization through the practice of Madhyamaka. The mahasiddhas of India are not restricted to those who gathered at Bodhgaya for a single ganachakra ceremony, later coming to be known as the "eighty-four mahasiddhas."[15] After that ganachakra ceremony, the enumeration of "eighty-four" mahasiddhas became very popular, but this does not mean there were only eighty-four. In India alone there were hundreds of thousands of great masters who practiced in this way; the names we havevlisted here are just a small percent of the total number of accomplished masters. Each one of these masters had many great disciples, and hence there are lots of authentic lineage holders. This is how the teaching lineage of Madhyamaka has remained vital until the present time. Many of the ancient masters came from the first monastic university in India, Nalanda. Later, sometime between the sixth and eighth centuries, another exceptional monastic university was established, called Vikramashila. As we have already seen, the first Tibetan monastery was Samye and the second was Sangphu.

The Svatantrika Madhyamaka of This Shedra

Throughout this shedra we will be using Mipham Rinpoche's commentary on Shantarakshita's *Madhyamkalankara*, which is called *Uma gyen gi namshe jamyang lama gyepai zhalung.*[16] Since the

Madhyamakalankara is a large book that contains many topics, we will not have time to discuss it in its entirety. Instead, we will use the text as a support for our teaching and study of Svatantrika Madhyamaka, exploring as much as possible in our discussion of this sublime philosophical school. Among all the commentaries on Shantarakshita's *Madhyamakalankara*, Mipham Rinpoche's is the largest and most detailed; it is actually one of the most thorough and precise commentaries in Tibetan Buddhist history.

Some of you may already know that the great master Tsongkhapa also began to write an extensive commentary on Shantarakshita's *Madhyamakalankara*. He started his text with a beautiful verse of praise to Shantarakshita, then began. But for some reason, he could not finish the commentary. Later, his disciple Gyaltsab Dharma Rinchen wrote what amounts to footnotes on Tsongkhapa's initial work, presenting his additional text under the title *Uma gyen gi jeyang* [*dBu ma rgyan gi brjed bang*]. Of course, this is not an extensive commentary.

We have seen that Lotsawa Loden Sherab and Chapa Chokyi Senge were great logicians and followers of Shantarakshita's philosophical system. In all likelihood they also wrote commentaries on the *Madhyamakalankara*. However, because they lived so long ago—in the eleventh and twelfth centuries—many of their works have disappeared. People hope to find commentaries by these great masters, but so far no additional works have been discovered. The teachings written by the great masters during this early period in Tibet (i.e. the eleventh and twelfth centuries) were transcribed by disciples and copied by hand—it takes a long time to write out these texts! And the Tibetan woodblock printing system is a relatively sophisticated and modern phenomenon that was not developed until around the 14th century. Even then, the woodblocks and prints took quite a long time to make. Thus, many works of the ancient masters have completely disappeared. For example, most of the works by Chapa Chokyi Senge, written in the beginning of the 12th century, are gone. I think a copy of a text by Chokyi Senge, providing an overview of Madhyamaka, was recently found in Tibet. Philippe Turenne obtained a copy of this text, which has not yet been published—we are sure that somebody will publish it soon. In any case, this is the reason why many ancient texts have disappeared.

Review of Svatantrika Madhyamaka Teachings

We will now begin to explore the teachings of Svatantrika Madhyamaka. Just last year, we consulted Longchenpa's teachings with respect to the four schools of Buddhism; this year we will consult his explanations of Mipham Rinpoche's commentary on the *Madhyamakalankara*.

From the Madhyamaka point of view, we must first consider the two truths. The two truths are extremely important since they comprise all objects of knowledge. But where were these truths taught and who taught them? They come directly from the teachings of Buddha Shakyamuni. There is a Mahayana sutra known as the *Sutra of the Meeting of Father and Son* [*Yab sras mjal ba'i mdo*] that recounts the story of how the Awakened One, after leaving his kingdom and attaining enlightenment, returned to meet his father the king. The Buddha is praised in this sutra: "Oh Omniscient One who knows everything! All-Knowing One, you taught the two truths, never before taught by anyone else in the world! And what are these two truths? They are relative and absolute truth." According to the teachings of Mahayana and Madhyamaka, many things exist both in the world and beyond it. Whatever can be conceived in the mind can be categorized into these classes of relative and absolute truth.

First, what is relative truth? Relative truth includes everything we think, hear, feel, and analyze. It includes everything we do. All phenomenal objects are classified under the label "relative truth." Relative truth is also known as that which is interrelated, functional, and connected to the mundane level. Consequently, different teachings such as the *Sutra of the Meeting of Father and Son* explain that relative truth can also be known as "relative truth of the mundane world" or "relative truth of samsara" (Skt. *loka-vyavahara-samvrti-satya*).

When we begin to analyze the exact meaning of relative truth and investigate the nature of phenomena we experience by means of feeling, hearing, seeing, and touching—in fact, all our activities—we do not find anything substantially solid to which we can grasp or cling. There is no solid existence behind these experiences: all evaporate into the state of emptiness, without a trace. This is known as "absolute truth."

Nevertheless, the two truths were never made into law by the Buddha. He never *ordered* us to believe in them. Even so, the two truths accurately describe the nature of reality. If we investigate reality on our own, trying to discover the essence of things by grasping on to objects as tangible—as things we can hold, touch, or feel—then the words of the Buddha appear to be false. We will say, "No, the two truths are not actually correct." However, as we continue investigate and discover the essence of objects, we eventually come to the realization that there is really nothing to find. In this case, we will see that the Buddha's words are true and that reality is as he described it. We will conclude that the two truths correctly describe the nature of reality as it is. Again, this is referred to as "absolute truth."

When we establish things according to how they appear to ordinary perception through hearing, touching, and feeling, this is relative truth. It includes conceptions such as "I like" and "I don't like"; "I am happy" and "I am not happy"; "this is good" and "that is bad"; "this is beautiful" and "that is not beautiful." All types of analysis, conceptualization, and everything we can express in words is relative truth just as it is. Yet when we look into each of these things, we cannot find any substantially solid basis behind them. This is known as "emptiness." The system of relative and absolute, which is actually two systems, is known as the view of Svatantrika Madhyamaka. Understanding reality in this way, one can experience relative truth exactly as it is, without grasping and clinging to things as substantial and solid. Such is the method for transcending limited conceptions and accepting reality exactly as it is, without overlapping the two truths, and without ignoring, judging, or imposing the two truths upon each other. We simply accept relative truth as it is and then move beyond it. This is taught by Svatantrika Madhyamaka.

When we say something is "beautiful" or "wonderful," this is relative truth. But let us think about what this "beautiful" thing really is. Where is this beauty? Does it lie in a mental state or in an object? To begin, we should examine where our concept of beauty comes from. Does this label exist in the mind—the subject—or in an object? Upon investigating in this way, we discover that there is nothing we can really hold or grasp on to; there is no substantially solid existing beauty. This is known as emptiness.

Similarly, when we speak of something as being "bad," this "badness" exists in terms of relative truth. Relatively speaking, bad is bad. But looking closer at the situation, we should try to find where badness resides. Does it reside in the perceiving subject or the perceived object? Where is this so-called "badness"? This name and label, this formation called "bad"—where is it? The more we think about and investigate the location of our conception, the more the whole thing evaporates. Not finding anything whatsoever is itself absolute truth. This is the philosophical view of the Svatantrika Madhyamaka school, put very simply and briefly.

"Svatantrika" is a Sanskrit word. *Sva* means "self" and *tantrika* comes from the word *tantra*, which means "continuation" or "self-continuation." Hence "Svatantrika" means "self-continuity." This means each and every object of relative truth is, in a way, self-continuing. On the relative level, everything is a chain of momentary instants, a self-continuing continuum. The first instant becomes the cause of the second instant, and the second instant is the result of the first. This is the self-continuation of conventional reality. On the absolute level, however, everything we see—all this self-continuation—is just an echo of great emptiness. Self-continuity is a sparkling chain of mirages, of emptiness. There is nothing anywhere that exists in a substantial or solid way. Svatantrika Madhyamaka encourages us to discover this self-continuing nature exactly as it is, both on the relative and absolute levels.

As we mentioned earlier, the Buddha taught about the nature as it is; he taught about the truth. But there is no imposition and no doctrine in the Buddha's teachings—there is nothing to *believe.* In Svatantrika Madhyamaka, we consider what is happening behind the scenes of mere appearances. We have to investigate and analyze what is really going on. In other words, the Buddha is talking to us and we are talking to the Buddha, to this nature. Simultaneously, we ourselves are *part* of the nature, so we have every right to investigate whether or not the teachings are true. Buddha Shakyamuni said this many times throughout the teachings. He said, "You should investigate, analyze, and discover whether or not my words are true. Only then should you accept or reject them." Therefore, we do not have to be overly polite or respectful when we talk about philosophical matters. Only when we agree with the teachings based on valid cognition—once the true nature has been legitimately established—do we have to accept them as true. If we persist in arguing after that point, we are merely lying and deceiving ourselves, ignoring truth as truth.

Benefits of the Nature As It Is

So, what are the benefits of this nature we have established through philosophical analysis? When we follow the true nature, we discover reality as it is: the Buddha. Once we find this nature, dualistic mind will no longer trick us. We all know that duality mind loves to fabricate and manipulate. It likes to grasp at phenomena, to doubt and hesitate. This is how duality mind operates. Our own self-deception has deceived us about the nature of reality from the beginning.

We have heard many times that all our labels, beliefs, and actions are simply the creations of our own minds. Nonetheless, we tend to believe in what we have created. We hold on to these phenomena, continually supporting and analyzing our mental constructions. Yet when we begin to investigate the nature of our beliefs by seeking their location, we find that none of them are substantially existent. None of them exist with any solidity. This is the nature of emptiness. Still, emptiness is not just a black hole something that helps us cover up or ignore the true nature. It is just the simple nature as it is. Our conceptions themselves create the ideas of permanence and impermanence, of "this" and "that," "up" and "down." And our duality mind then clings to these conceptions. Everything we can name is the creation of duality mind! It is this very situation we must investigate and analyze.

Again, not finding anything upon looking is referred to as "emptiness." The Tibetan word for emptiness is *tonpa nyid* [*stong pa nyid*], but it is also called *denpe tongpa* [*bden pe stong pa*], which means "no solid nature exists." Emptiness, the absence of a solid nature, is pervasive. Nothing has a substantial nature, regardless of whether we believe a given thing to be good or bad. Even enlightenment has no solid nature. This means we cannot say "samsara is empty but nirvana is not empty," or "samsara has no solid nature, but nirvana has a solid nature." That is not what the Buddha taught: samsara has no solid nature; nirvana has no solid nature; samsara is emptiness; and nirvana is emptiness. For this reason, in his *Prajnaparamita* teachings, the Blessed One often said, "There is something even higher and deeper than buddhahood, which goes beyond any concept such as 'Buddha is empty, or enlightenment is empty.'" Enlightenment has no solid nature and nirvana also has no solid nature. Then what is really going on? Appearances are just a magical display—they are magic.

This is why we chant the *Heart Sutra* every day when we get together. In this teaching, the Awakened One says, "No eye, no ear, no nose, no tongue, no body…no wisdom, no five aggregates, no twelve nidhanas, no eighteen dhatus, no twelve links of dependent origination, no path, no journey, no wisdom, no loss, no gain, no decrease, and no increase." What is the meaning of this? When the Buddha taught in this way, he had not become a cuckoo—he wasn't crazy! Still, if he said this under normal circumstances, people surely would have thought he was crazy and completely out of order. This is due to the fact that we believe, grasp, cling, and hold on to our conceptions. As a result we constantly suffer. Buddha Shakyamuni released all conceptual boundaries and traps. His teachings bring us to the state of total freedom which results from discovering the essence of the nature as it is. This is the central philosophy of Svatantrika Madhyamaka. Once more, it means that every aspect of what we normally consider to be our "selves" is empty: the self has no solid nature, the eye has no solid nature, and the nose has no solid nature, etc. Put another way, the eye is self-emptiness, the nose is self-emptiness, consciousness is self-emptiness, and the entire universe—including samsara and nirvana—is self-empty.

By discovering the nature as it is, we will actually *be* in the natural state. This is known as "meditation." Meditation is nothing more than maintaining awareness of the nature as it is, without extreme views. Simply resting in the natural state, we discover meditation—such is the authentic view of the nature. There is only one true nature; therefore, the views of Madhyamaka, Mahamudra, and Dzogpa Chenpo are not contradictory. The same is true for the *Chod* practice of Machig Labdron, which we have had the opportunity to discuss in the past. Additionally, discovering the nature as it is will pacify the sufferings of duality, as in the *Shije* practice of Padampa Sangye. The great master Padampa Sangye's *Shije* teachings are referred to as "the pacification lineage teachings" because by practicing them, one pacifies the suffering that results from duality mind and its fabrications. The various kinds of suffering are just part of the game of duality. By discovering the nature and maintaining this discovery, one attains realization. This great realization is known as *Lamdre*, or "path and result," according to the teachings of the Sakya school of Tibetan Buddhism. Due to practicing these teachings, one achieves the result that was sought on the level of relative truth.

We should understand that Madhyamaka is not just some kind of intellectual game. It represents an essential practice and meditation. Within Buddhism, study, contemplation, and meditation on the Buddha's teachings must be united so that one doesn't fall into the scapegoat of intellectualism or skepticism. We have to nourish ourselves and absorb the teachings, so that we can expand our realization, love, kindness, and thoughts related with the goodness of the natural state, thus breaking through the boundaries of duality. Then we will really begin to reveal our own true beauty as it is. This is the purpose of all the philosophical teachings that were laid out and taught by the many accomplished and realized masters we mentioned earlier.

As we continue our discussion of Madhyamaka, we should continually restrengthen our beautiful motivation of bodhichitta, thinking, "All living beings would like to achieve enlightenment, and I wish to lead them all to this state. In order to do so, I am going to study, contemplate, and meditate on the profound meaning of the *Prajnaparamita* and Madhyamaka." It is always important to keep this beautiful motivation in our hearts.

Madhyamaka Is Beyond Conception

In general, "Madhyamaka" is known as *Uma* in Tibetan. It has been commonly translated into English as "the Middle Way" or "the Middle Path," but it may also be translated as "center." But this does not refer to a center with boundaries—it is a center completely free from all limits and territory. Anything with boundaries is not considered to be Madhyamaka, the Middle Way. In a way, this "middle" refers to the "heart of the true nature." Buddha Shakyamuni taught again and again that if we have any grasping, clinging, or holding, we are not practicing Madhyamaka. Grasping and holding are forms of extremism; they are at the edge. So if we grasp to notions such as "existence," we are not engaging in Madhyamaka. Likewise, holding on to any notion of "nonexistence" is not Madhyamaka. Nor is grasping to the notions of "both existing and non-existing" and "neither existing nor non-existing." We have to release every aspect of dualistic conception, freeing ourselves from all extremes. Studying, contemplating, and meditating in this way is known as Madhyamaka.

The simple way to understand Madhyamaka is to recognize that it is entirely beyond all conceptions. When you have the view which is free from conceptions, and you behold the state devoid of all grasping and duality, you are experiencing an authentic glimpse of the Madhyamaka view. Truly, grasping and clinging have nothing to do with Madhyamaka. For this reason, the words "center," "Madhyamaka," and "Middle Way" are just names that point out the profound nature and usher us into recognition of the nature as it is. This is a brief description of the meaning of the word "Madhyamaka."

Madhyamaka and *Prajnaparamita*

When we investigate Madhyamaka, we discover that there are many different categories and divisions through which we can explore this philosophical school. In this shedra we are presenting an overview of the entire scope of the Madhyamaka teachings, as if gazing out from the peak of a mountain in a panoramic view of the entirety of the Buddha's teachings. From this perspective, we can see the Madhyamaka of the sutras as well as the Madhyamaka of the tantras; it is possible to divide Madhyamaka in this way. According to the Madhyamaka of the sutras, there are two Umas: scriptural Madhyamaka and commentarial Madhyamaka, the second of which is more more with texts, teachings, and books. These books explain the teachings of Buddha Shakyamuni, including the commentaries made by great masters who expounded the doctrine of the Awakened One. In Tibetan, we call these *Ka Uma* and *Shang Uma*, respectively—that is, the Uma of the Buddha's speech (i.e. scriptural) and the Uma of the commentaries on his oral teachings.

Scriptural Madhyamaka refers to the three seminal teachings given by the Blessed One, as described in Sutra Mahayana: the first, second, and third turnings of the wheel of Dharma. Of these seminal teachings, the first turning of the wheel of Dharma is not considered to be a Madhyamaka teaching; the entire second turning *is* considered to be a teaching on Madhyamaka; and the third turning contains teachings on both Madhyamaka and other subjects. Thus, for the most part, the third turning of the wheel of Dharma is connected with Madhyamaka. To summarize, the entire second turning and most of the third turning are Madhyamaka teachings.

However, the Buddha did not specifically use Madhyamaka terminology in his teachings, only occasionally using related terms. Instead, the Blessed One explained Madhyamaka in the language of his *Prajnaparamita* teachings, which were given throughout the second and third turnings of the wheel of Dharma. But what is the true meaning of "prajnaparamita"? As most of you know, it is roughly translated into English as "wisdom that goes beyond" or "transcendent wisdom." Yet within the context of *Prajnaparamita*, the word "wisdom" does not refer to intellectual knowledge, but rather to wisdom without territory, wisdom completely beyond conception. This transcendent wisdom is impartial, clearly and perfectly understanding the truth nature on both the relative and absolute levels. By realizing this nature we "go beyond." And what do we go beyond? Duality. This is the essence of the *Prajnaparamita* teachings. The practice and meditation of transcendent wisdom leads us to that which transcends duality altogether. In other cases, "prajnaparamita" is understood as something that goes beyond samsara and nirvana. Nevertheless, more specifically it relates with "going beyond duality." When we transcend duality, we discover the innate nature as it is. So, the Buddha generally explained Madhyamaka by way of his *Prajnaparamita* teachings.

The great master Nagarjuna used Madhyamaka terminology to explain the Buddha's teachings on *Prajnaparamita*. This language was established in his famous work entitled the *Mula-madhyamaka-prajna*. So, this text and those that followed it widely use Madhyamaka terminology to explain and explore the profound meaning of the

Prajnaparamita. Asanga, another exceptional master, also applied Madhyamaka vocabulary to the Supreme Teacher's *Prajnaparamita* discourses. In this way, Nagarjuna and Asanga were the two principal masters who intensely explored *Prajnaparamita*—in a pointed and accessible way—so that everybody could understand and learn how to practice on transcendent wisdom. The *Prajnaparamita* teachings are often said to be very profound, vast, and deep; many masters describe them as being "as deep as an ocean, as vast as the sky, and as infinite as space." Such are the common descriptions of the *Perfection of Wisdom Sutras*. It is difficult even for mature, intellectual people to understand their meaning. Therefore, it is extremely fortunate that Nagarjuna and Asanga clarified the profound and essential meaning of these teachings.

Prajnaparamita is often described in terms of its "direct meaning" and "hidden meaning." The direct meaning of *Prajnaparamita* was widely taught by Nagarjuna in his *Mula-madhyamaka-prajna*, whereas the hidden meaning was discovered by Asanga. Asanga wrote many famous works throughout his lifetime, including the *Five Treatises of Maitreya*, which were actually taught by Maitreya and written down by Asanga himself.[17] Because their teachings are so profound, these two remarkable masters—Nagarjuna and Asanga—are often known as the "great suns of Buddhism," or "the sun and moon of the Buddha's teachings." As we have seen, Buddha Shakyamuni predicted their arrival as well as the arrival of many others, but it would take too much time to mention them all here. It is not accidental that Nagarjuna and Asanga are so renowned; actually, they were so special and powerful that Buddhist philosophy in general, and the Madhyamaka and *Prajnaparamita* teachings in particular, have continued in an unbroken lineage until the present.

Three major Buddhist philosophical schools developed as a result of Nagarjuna's *Mula-madhyamaka-prajna*, his exposition of Madhyamaka as the deep meaning of the *Prajnaparamita*. These are known as Sautrantika Madhyamaka (Sutra Middle Way school),

Yogachara Madhyamaka (Mind Only Middle Way school), and Prasangika Madhyamaka (Consequentialist Middle Way school). Although other Madhyamaka schools also developed, these three are principal among them all. For instance, the Vaibashika Madhyamaka school—associated with the Hinanyana school of the Vaibashikas—also emerged after Nagarjuna's great work. Sautrantika Madhyamaka emerged with Bhavaviveka; Yogachara Madhyamaka emerged with the cofounder of Tibetan Buddhism, our own great master Shantarakshita; and, finally, Prasangika Madhyamaka emerged with Chandrakirti. Regarding these three schools, the first two are classified as Svatantrika Madhyamaka, whereas Chandrakirti's teachings are classified as Prasangika Madhyamaka. Therefore, the simplest way to classify Madhyamaka is according to the Svatantrika-Prasangika (or Rangyupa-Tangyurpa) distinction.

Questions and Answers

Question: Madhyamaka and the Hinayana seem to be very different from one another? How are they related to one another?

Answer: Madhyamaka is referred to as the "Middle Way" in part because it incorporates teachings from the Hinayana all the way up to Dzogchen. Yet there is a slight difference between the Madhyamaka as it appears in Hinayana Buddhism and Madhyamaka philosophy itself. Buddhism often speaks about "view," "conduct, " and "meditation." Our conduct should be Madhyamaka conduct, our view should be Madhyamaka view, and our meditation should be Madhyamaka meditation.

The Hinayana view is related with Madhyamaka, so we often speak of the "Hinayana view of Madhyamaka." Once we let go of the notion of a substantial or permanent ego—a defining characteristic of Hinayana Buddhism—we are freed from the extreme of permanence. Yet although we are freed from the mistaken conception of an ego, everything functions without any blockage. But what is left when we drop the extreme of permanence? Egolessness; we are left with egolessness. This direct experience of egolessness frees us from nihilism. In this way, the Hinayana view is also a Madhyamaka view. The view of egolessness is actually the view of both the Vaibhashikas and Sautrantikas, including the Pratyekabuddhas.

Madhyamaka conduct is also free from extremes, since it does not lean towards indulgence (i.e. luxury) or asceticism. In other words, Madhyamaka does not engage in the hardships of asceticism, nor the greed that is often related with luxury. This is the conduct of the Middle Way.

Finally, the view of Cittamatra (Mind Only) is self-awareness free from duality, which also releases us from the extreme view of permanence. Still, because the luminosity and radiance of awareness is ever-present, we do not fall into the trap of nihilism. In this way, the view of the Cittamatrins is also a Madhyamaka view.

Question: What does "contemplation" really mean?

Answer: Contemplation refers to investigating and analyzing the teachings we have received. It is important to inquire into the deep meaning of the teachings and try to make some sense of them. In general, all living beings have some form of contemplation wisdom, which basically means they are free from doubt. There are many things about which we have no doubt: For example, we tend to believe in causes, conditions, and results. Upon seeing a result, everybody knows that it is produced from causes and conditions. Nobody questions this. Once we have developed this certainty, that is known as "contemplation," since true contemplation is knowledge free from doubt. The fact that results develop from causes and conditions is known as the true nature of illusory, or relative truth. But it is not as though somebody forced us to believe in conventional reality. It's very simple: When perfect causes and conditions come together, results are produced.

However, when we aren't aware of the causes and conditions that give rise to a particular result, we must thoroughly investigate the relationship between cause and result at a deeper level. This is also known as contemplation. Contemplation does not mean we merely hear the teachings; we have to carefully investigate and analyze them to discover their deep meaning. Once more, contemplation means we develop certainty wisdom, about which we don't have any doubt. That's it! In a way the contemplation guidelines are very simple.

Sometimes, in the Tibetan monasteries, a younger student or junior khenpo would review the teachings given by a senior khenpo. He might go over the teachings with the other monks. Perhaps they would study the teachings once or twice, and then get together and encourage one another. They often debated, asking each other difficult questions. This, too, is contemplation. Also, we can read through different Dharma books and ask a lot of questions about what we have discovered; there are many different angles through which we can view the teachings. In this way we will develop the wisdom of contemplation.

Rangtong and Shentong

After their introduction from India, these two philosophical systems became extremely powerful and popular in Tibet. Sometime between the 14th and 16th centuries, further divisions of Madhyamaka appeared, including the *Rangtong* ("self-emptiness") and *Shentong* ("other-emptiness") schools. "Self-emptiness" and "other-emptiness" are rough English translations of the Tibetan, but it is more accurate to simply refer to them as Rangtong and Shentong.

Generally speaking, the division between Rangtong and Shentong is based upon a very subtle point concerning buddha-nature. Everyone agrees that buddha-nature is inherent in every living being, without exception. However, although the Rangtongpas believe buddha-nature is continuously inherent since beginningless time until enlightenment, they claim that its nature is empty, or self-empty. In other words, buddha-nature is empty of *itself*. This is the Rangtong view.

In contrast, *Shentong* means "empty of other." The Shentongpas assert that buddha-nature is already enlightened, already in the fully-developed wisdom state. They explain that, even though buddha-nature is in this state right now, we do not recognize it at the present time due to temporary obscurations and defilements. Basically, Shentongpas believe that enlightenment is immediately present when buddha-nature is emptied of all things *not* buddha-nature Thus, they teach the importance of emptying and releasing buddha-nature from the obscuring habitual patterns, from all negativities and defilements, at which point enlightment is right there. This is why the Shentong school is called "empty of other." We have now completed our brief overview and general introduction to the different Madhyamaka systems.

Svatantrika Madhyamaka

We will now proceed to discuss the teachings of Svatantrika Madhyamaka itself, specifically the Yogachara Madhyamaka school as it was taught by the great master Shantarakshita. Shantarakshita's *Madhyamakalankara* is the root text of the Yogachara Madhyamaka school; in a way, it is the foundation of the entire Svatantrika philosophy. We will study this text according to Longchenpa's teachings on the Yogachara Svatantrika Madhyamaka school, in addition to Mipham Rinpoche's commentary on Shantarakshita's work. As we have said throughout these teachings, there are no big differences between the various Madhyamaka traditions, and the differences that do exist have to do with very subtle points. The correct practice of any of these traditions will lead us to enlightenment, so there is also no difference between the schools at the level of result. Nonetheless, regarding their application, or method of practice, each of the Madhyamaka schools is unique.

Khenchen Bodhisattva, Shantarakshita

Shantarakshita's *Madhyamakalankara* has been translated into English along with Mipham Rinpoche's famous commentary. By reading these texts, we can see how special Shantarakshita really was. We all know that Khenchen Shantarakshita was the cofounder of Tibetan Buddhism, but his greatness was not limited to this achievement alone: He was also a highly accomplished master, an enlightened being, mahasiddha, great scholar, logician, debater, and thinker. His fame is in no way coincidental. As Mipham Rinpoche explains in his commentary, Shantarakshita was also predicted by Buddha Shakyamuni.

It is said that Shantarakshita lived for over nine hundred years; according to his own explanation, he spent nine generations waiting for the appearance of King Trisong Deutsen. Shantarakshita remarked that in a past life, Guru Padmasambhava, King Trisong Deutsen, and himself all made aspiration prayers that in the future they would together bring the Buddhadharma to a place where it hadn't previously existed. When Shantarakshita first met King Trisong Deutsen, he took firm hold of the king's hands and shook them as he spoke, "I have waited nine generations for this moment. Do you remember our ancient commitment? Do you remember?" King Trisong Deutsen answered, "I can vaguely remember, though I don't remember clearly because I have not meditated long enough."

It is said that Shantarakshita repeatedly travelled back and forth between India and Tibet—and even went to China—to spread the Dharma. The fact that he could postpone his death for nine generations and live for nine hundred years demonstrates his extremely high level of realization—truly, he was an enlightened master. As normal people, we generally live for seventy or eighty years before ending up in a nursing home, if we are lucky! Most likely we would experience many difficulties and great suffering at the end of such a long life. But Shantarakshita never underwent these hindrances. He simply waited for the right time to be born and then established Buddhism in Tibet. Finally, having left his legacy and fulfilled his commitments, he departed. Many emanations of Shantarakshita appeared in later times due to his strong commitment while chanting aspiration prayers.

The glory of Shantarakshita cannot be overstated. He was one of the most accomplished masters of Tibetan Buddhism, particularly in terms of the Tibetan monastic institution. It was Shantarakshita himself who founded monasticism in the Land of Snows. Furthermore, the example Shantarakshita offered as a role model and the teachings and messages he delivered are still alive for today's practitioners of Tibetan Buddhism, not only in Tibet, but also in the bordering countries of China, Nepal, Bhutan, and Mongolia. The great master's teachings travelled far and wide, and we continue to practice his lineage teachings and benefit from his blessings.

Many teachings state that Shantarakshita was an emanation of

Vajrapani. When he first arrived in Tibet, the great bodhisattva had some difficulty establishing the Buddhist tradition due to the many negative and destructive forces of invisible beings throughout the region. In reality, however, Shantarakshita had no trouble subduing these beings; he only made it appear so because of his ancient pact with Guru Padmasambhava and King Trisong Deutsen. It was necessary for all three teachers to spread the Buddhadharma in Tibet, so Shantarakshita used the pretext of difficulty subduing the negative forces to encourage King Trisong Deutsen to invite Guru Padmasambhava to Tibet, stating that Padmasambhava would easily subdue the obstacles. The great bodhisattva was using skillful means to create auspicious circumstances for the country of Tibet. He definitely had the ability to pacify the evil spirits of the region—this is why he was renowned as an emanation of Vajrapani. Additionally, Guru Padmasambhava was renowned as an emanation of Buddha Amitabha, and Trisong Deutsen was renowned as an emanation of Manjushri. Hence one often hears that three buddhas—Vajrapani, Amitabha, and Manjushri—came together to establish Dharma in the Land of Snows.

There were many lineage holders of Shantarakshita's teachings, including Kamalashila, Acharya Haribhadra, Dharmamitra, Arya Vimuktisena, and Abhayakara Gupta. Each of these teachers was a lineage holder of the Yogachara Madhyamaka school and a follower of Shantarakshita's philosophical system. As we discussed earlier, the twenty-five disciples of Guru Padmasambhava also adhered to Shantarakshita's philosophical system.

Longchenpa and Mipham Rinpoche

The great masters Longchen Rabjam Drime Oser (Longchenpa) and Mipham Jamyang Namgyal Gyatso were predicted both in the discourses of Buddha Shakyamuni and in many termas of Guru Padmasambhava. As foretold, they became exceptional masters. Although their degree of realization was equal to that of the Blessed

One and Guru Rinpoche, they were extremely humble, simple, and gentle, as if they were ordinary human beings. Longchenpa and Mipham Rinpoche continually maintained these qualities of modesty, humility, respect, and appreciation, along with devotion and pure perception throughout their lives. In fact, they possessed all the good qualities of conduct we can name—including loving-kindness and renunciation—despite the fact they had achieved unsurpassed scholarship and ultimate realization.

Relative and Absolute Truth

We will continue our exploration of Madhyamaka with a discussion of relative and absolute truth. The great Longchenpa describes "five categories of explanation" associated with the two truths. The first category is known as the "object of valid cognition," which is the basis of the two-truth division. This refers to all mere objects of knowledge perceived with valid cognition. Without such a basis, the two truths could not be differentiated in the first place.

The second category of explanation is the "purpose of the divisions." In order to dispel mistaken perceptions about the nature as it is, it is important to clarify why we distinguish between relative and absolute truth. This second category has four subdivisions: the first two relate with mistaken perceptions about the two truths, whereas the last two are accurate descriptions of the two truths used by different Madhyamaka masters.

Refuting the Sameness of the Two Truths

Some people claim that relative and absolute truth are simply two different names that refer to a single object. For example, the object we refer to as the "sun" in English is known as *dawa* in Tibetan and *sol* in Spanish. This view is incorrect; relative and absolute truth are not the same, nor are they different names for the same object. Four logical fallacies result from asserting the sameness of the two truths.

1. Error One

First, if we were to hold the belief that relative and absolute truth are the same, they would both be absolute, and consequently we would make many logical errors. Logically speaking, if relative and absolute truths were the same, everybody would recognize absolute truth immediately after experiencing relative truth: Since anyone can perceive relative truth, this truth would simultaneously be understood as absolute in the very moment of experiencing conventional reality. It is commonly accepted that upon seeing absolute truth one becomes enlightened, it logically follows that everybody who experiences relative truth would instantly be enlightened. But such is not the case at all. This is the biggest error that results from assuming relative and absolute truths to be the same.

2. Error Two

Second, if the two truths were the same, there would have to be the same number of relative and absolute truths: mountains, water, tables, and cups are all examples of relative truth, so there would have to be just as many absolute truths. Still, by definition there cannot be many absolute truths. This is the second error that results from failing to distinguish between the two truths.

3. Error Three

The third logical fallacy is connected with emotions. The emotions of sentient beings naturally arise along with the many appearances of relative truth, swinging back and forth between extremes of happiness and sorrow. In contrast, the recognition of absolute truth does not cause emotions to increase and fluctuate between opposite poles; instead, it leads to the state of perfect enlightenment. So, sentient beings are constantly deluded by relative phenomenal appearances and so experience many negative emotions and suffering due misperceiving this conventional reality. On the other hand, they attain perfect enlightenment upon recognizing the absolute state and maintaining that recognition. Thus, absolute and relative truth are not the same.

4. Error Four

Finally, if the two truths were the same, why would we make the distinction between relative and absolute in the first place? What would be the purpose of creating two absolute truths? These four arguments are used to refute the view that relative and absolute truths are identical. Thus, we have to accept that the two truths are different. We will later use four similar points to refute the mistaken assumption that the two truths are completely separate. The Omniscient Longchenpa used four reasonings to refute both erroneous views: (1) believing the two truths to be identical, and (2) believing the two truths to be completely separate. From these reasonings, we come to understand that absolute and relative truths are *not* the same; rather, they are two different aspects of the same nature.

If relative and absolute truth are not the same, how should we perceive them? We should perceive them as though witnessing a magic show. Actually, the two truths *are* magical. Relative truth exists conventionally, but the moment we investigate it, we find that it no longer exists in the way we normally perceive it—it is simply a magical display. This is why, in the *Prajnaparamita Sutra*, the Buddha said, "On the level of reality, the nature is neither true nor untrue." The nature is beyond the dualistic concepts of "true" and "untrue." As long as we cling to these notions, we will not behold the nature of reality. At the level of meditation, or realization, we must recognize everything as great emptiness, totally beyond all false dichotomies and conceptual fabrications. From this perspective, everything is like the blue sky, or space, without any essential or solid nature. Simultaneously, on the relative level of experience, everything should be understood as a continually arising magical display.

Refuting the Separateness of the Two Truths

We have just refuted the mistaken notion that the two truths are the same. Now we will use four additional reasonings to refute the mistaken notion that the two truths are completely different. This is the second subdivision of Longchenpa's second category of explanation.

1. Error One

Some people claim that relative and absolute truth are completely different, just as a horse is different from a cow. This view is also incorrect. First, it is commonly agreed that complete realization of absolute truth leads directly to enlightenment. But if relative and absolute truths were totally distinct, one would not achieve enlightenment even upon realizing absolute truth. After reaching this so-called "enlightenment," one would have to search for the nature of relative truth as well. By definition, such a realization would be partial and limited.

2. Error Two

Second, if the two truths were completely separate, what would the authentic nature of absolute truth be? If absolute truth did not actually include the nature of relative truth, what would make it "absolute"? Furthermore, where would absolute truth come from is the two truths were separate? And how would recognizing that things don't substantially exist benefit us at all? Such an understanding of the insubstantiality (or interdependence) of phenomena would be totally disconnected from emptiness. So why did the Buddha teach, "Form is emptiness, emptiness is form"? If the two truths were separate, realizing absolute truth would make absolutely no difference in terms of conventional reality.

3. Error Three

Third, if relative and absolute truth were two different things, there would be no point in realizing the relative absence of an ego. How would this help, since understanding egolessness on the relative level could never lead to realization of absolute truth? Similarly, there wouldn't be any benefit to understanding that objects have no substantial nature. For instance, recognizing that objects have no substantially solid existence—i.e. a vase has no essential "vaseness" outside of imputed labels—would not help us understand the absolute nature, or great emptiness, because relative and absolute are assumed to be completely separate. Relative and absolute realization would have two different objects of perception.

4. Error Four

Fourth, if the two truths were distinct, a perfect realization of absolute truth would not lead to enlightenment, given that one would still lack a complete realization of relative truth. One would not be omniscient. Having achieved absolute realization, we would still lack understanding on the relative level. Thus, we would have to learn all relative truths and would experience all kinds of emotions due to grasping, since understanding the absolute would not help us understand conventional reality in the least. Relative understanding would correspond to an entirely distinct object of knowledge, separate from absolute truth. Again, we would have to develop realization on the conventional level, continually experiencing ignorance and suffering. For all these reasons, relative and absolute truth cannot be separate from one another, nor can they refer to the same thing.

What, then, is the actual relationship between the two truths? The basis of the division between the two truths is an object of knowledge. And all objects of knowledge, including everything that can be conceptualized or imagined, can be divided according to the two truths. As quoted in Longchenpa's text, the two truths are not one, yet they are not two, either. This is the third subdivision of the second category: The two truths are two different aspects of the same nature. Put differently, they are one meaning with two aspects. Lastly, other Madhyamaka masters explained the actual nature of the two truths in a slightly different way. They said, "One exists due to the absence of the other." Similarly, nighttime is absent when daytime is here; to say "yes" implies the absence of "no"; and to say that one thing is here logically implies that its opposite is absent.

Valid Cognition and the Two Truths

Who observes these two truths? None other than our own intelligence, our own minds. Our minds observe both relative and absolute truth. Yet mind has many different aspects. For example, there is a correct aspect of mind and an incorrect aspect of mind. When we see an accurate picture of relative truth, our intelligence is known as "accurate intelligence." In Tibetan, this is known as *chog tsema* [*mchog tshad ma*], which means "true mind" or "accurate mind," as well as "valid knowledge" or "valid cognition." Valid cognition may examine either relative or absolute truth, and it is this same valid cognition that observes and judges objects in relation to relative and absolute truth.

There are two different types of relative truth: "mistaken relative truth" and "accurate relative truth." Accurate relative truth itself has two divisions: "pure accurate relative truth" and "impure accurate relative truth." Pure accurate relative truth is only experienced by buddhas and bodhisattvas and relates with wisdom, whereas impure accurate relative truth is the perception that arises during times of heavy obscuration.[18] Impure accurate relative truth is still considered valid, because this impurity is not due to any defect in our eyes, nor is our consciousness working improperly due to circumstances. Such view is true as it is, and thus it is referred to as "valid." In other words, impure accurate relative truth is not based upon delusion due to specific circumstances such as cataracts or other defects. It is called "accurate" because it is fresh, contextual, immediate knowledge acquired through valid cognition. In this respect, it is true.

In fact, since impure accurate relative truth is experienced with valid cognition, we cannot really call it "impure." According the philosophical teachings of the Nyingma school, however, it is known as "valid cognition of the impure" or "impure valid cognition." Nyingmapas divide valid cognition into two classes: impure valid cognition and pure valid cognition. Put differently, they are called "impure cognition of the valid" and "pure cognition of the valid." Of course, impure valid cognition is very important. It is mainly through this type of valid cognition that we operate in the world. For instance, the famous Buddhist logician Dharmakirti based his teachings, including the *Pramanavartika*, the *Nyayabindu*, and the *Pramanaviniscaya*, on this type of impure valid cognition, although he does not specifically call it "impure." Dharmakirti simply calls it "direct valid cognition," which is *pratyaksa-pramana* in Sanskrit and *ngon sum tsema* [*mngon sum tshad ma*] in Tibetan.

On the other hand, "pure valid cognition" is the valid cognition of enlightened beings and great bodhisattvas. Their valid cognition is quite different than that of ordinary, heavily obscured beings. This is why the Nyingma masters divided valid cognition into two categories. Similarly, the *Guyhagarbha Tantra* describes two kinds of "valid cognition of relative truth." In these Vajrayana teachings, for example, the five aggregates are said to be the five dhyani buddhas, while the five elements are said to be the five female buddhas. Additionally, the Vajrayana teachings regard the entire universe as an enlightened mandala, in which the phenomenal realm and all living beings are all perfectly pure from the beginning. Such teachings reflect an understanding based on pure valid cognition. We don't presently recognize the enlightened state of the aggregates and elements—nor do we experience the entire universe as an enlightened mandala—due to our habitual obscurations; currently we only have access to impure valid cognition.

The distinction between pure and impure valid cognition means that the same object can be perceived in two different ways. First, we should determine whether a valid cognition—such as the five dhyani buddhas and the five female buddhas—is related with absolute or relative truth. This pure valid cognition, for example, is still characterized as relative truth. Just because we do not normally perceive reality in this way does not mean it is untrue. We don't see relative truth as it is perceived with pure valid cognition only because our present valid cognition is limited, and limited valid cognition cannot perceive the objects of unlimited valid cognition. At this point we should qualify that Svatantrika Madhyamaka itself does not explain pure valid cognition, so, in a way, we have sidetracked the issue. Svatantrika Madhyamaka explains only the valid cognition that is perceived by everybody.

Meaning of the Two Truths

We have completed the second category of explanation, which discusses the purpose of distinguishing between the two truths. Now we will begin to teach on the third category of explanation—the word meaning—by discussing the terms "relative" and "absolute."

In Sanskrit, the word for "relative truth" is *samvrti-satya. Samvrti* means "blockage," "veil," or "curtain," but it can also mean "artificial." This word signifies a layer or cover that prevents one from seeing what is really present. And what is being obscured? Samvrti-satya is actually absolute truth covered up by delusion. But if relative perception is based in delusion, why do we describe it with the term *satya*, or truth? The veil of conventional reality is referred to as "true" because not only do I perceive this covering, but you perceive it as well. In fact, everybody sees the same relative cover; we all see the same things, which appear to be very real and true even though they are actually delusion. Thus, relative truth is named samvrti-satya despite the fact it is not actually true.

The great early translators of Tibet rendered this Sanskrit term—samvrti-satya—as *kun dzob denpa* [*kun rdzob bden pa*] in Tibetan. *Kun* means "all" and is the equivalent of the Sanskrit prefix *sam*, while *dzob* refers to the Sanskrit word *vrti*, signifying something that is artificial, like a scarecrow or mask. Vrti can also refer to an illusion. So, *dzob* is like a mask or delusion, something artificial. There are many Tibetan synonyms for the word dzob, including *nyingpo medpa* [*snying po med pa*] and *yamala* [*ya ma brla*]. All these terms indicate that relative truth is not absolute—it is not the *real* truth. Therefore, the great Longchenpa said, "Everything we perceive is like a dream image—illusory, despite appearing to be real."

Let us now investigate the term "absolute truth." Absolute truth is called *paramartha-satya* in Sanskrit. The word *parama* means "supreme," but can also be translated as "unsurpassable" or "ultimate." *Artha* means "meaning," "purpose," or "goal." So, *paramartha* denotes "supreme meaning" or "absolute meaning." It can also mean "supreme goal," "unsurpassable goal," "unsurpassable meaning," or even "absolute goal." As we have already seen, absolute truth is the undeluded realization of valid cognition; it is valid cognition of the true nature as it is. Hence, the term paramartha-satya signifies undeluded realization of the absolute nature of reality. In Tibetan, the word for absolute truth is *don dam denpa* [*don dam bden pa*]. Again, the component parts of this word are not arbitrary, but have been used intentionally to convey and establish a certain meaning. This concludes our brief teaching on the word meaning of relative and absolute truth. We have now covered three of the five categories of explanation: (1) the object of valid cognition, (2) the purpose of distinguishing between the two truths, and (3) the word meaning of relative and absolute truth.

In terms of the fourth category of explanation, it is unnecessary to have more than two divisions of truth. This is the proper way to classify the nature of reality, since all object are encompassed, included, and encapsulated within the categories of relative and absolute truth. The fifth category of explanation is related to the fourth; there would be no purpose in having more than two truths. On the other hand, anything less than these two truths would not encompass all objects of knowledge. For this reason, distinguishing between the two truths allows us to precisely include *all* objects of knowledge, and thus it is the correct way to characterize reality.

Jnanagarbha's *Two Truths*

Within relative truth it is helpful to understand two divisions that were clearly distinguished by the famous master Jnanagarbha, the teacher of Shantarakshita. In his Madhyamaka teaching known as the *Two Truths*, Jnanagarbha states that relative truth is perceived with either false valid cognition or true valid cognition. These two valid cognitions encompass two kinds of relative truth: mistaken relative truth and accurate relative truth. As we saw earlier, accurate relative truth is truth undeluded by interference due to (defects in) the six senses. Anything experienced in this way is known as "pure valid cognition" or accurate relative truth.

And what is false valid cognition, or mistaken relative truth? One example of false valid cognition is seeing the color white as if it were yellow due to the condition of jaundice. "False valid cognition" implies that one of the six senses—in this case the eye—is defective on account of a disease or disorder. Similarly, when a person sees double images or "hairs in the sky" due to cataracts, he or she is experiencing mistaken relative truth. While it is not denied that the person is actually experiencing these deceptive images—which is why they are classified as "valid cognition"—these perceptions are not considered to be true on the relative level, because they are not perceived by everyone else. This is why false valid cognition is classified as "mistaken relative truth."

The Four Categories of Relative Truth

Svatantrika Madhyamaka subdivides relative truth into four categories. (1) The first category is that everything arises from causes and conditions, and without these causes and conditions phenomena cannot arise. For example, barley arises when seeds are planted in the earth and those seeds are nourished with water and sunlight. (2) Second, phenomena give rise to other phenomena that share similar characteristics. Take seeds, for example: rice seeds will develop into plants that produce more rice seeds, and flowers will eventually give rise to other flowers, etc. (3) Third, phenomena function in accordance with their appearance. For instance, fire is perceived as hot and tables are perceived as being able to support books and other objects. True to their appearances, fire *is* hot, and tables *are* able to support objects. (4) Fourth, upon deeply investigating phenomena, one does not find them to be substantially, truly existent; it is almost as if they dissolve before our eyes. This is how Svatantrika Madhyamaka subdivides relative phenomena into the "four identities," or "four identifying qualities of relative truth."

Two Divisions of Absolute Truth

Svatantrika Madhyamaka also divides absolute truth in two ways. These are roughly translated into English as "countable absolute truth" and "uncountable absolute truth." In Tibetan, they are called *nam drangpai don dam denpa* [*rnam grangs pa'i don dam bden pa*] and *nam drang ma yin pai don dam denpa* [*rnam grangs ma yin pa'i don dam bden pa*], respectively. Countable absolute truth refers to the idea of absolute truth held in the imagination, such as "everything is emptiness" and "the nature is unborn," as well as the very concepts of "emptiness," "unborn," and "impermanence." While these concepts are true, they are still based in the imagination. For this reason they are known as countable absolute truth; in other words, we could say they refer to absolute truth rooted in partiality. They are not completely true.

And what is uncountable absolute truth? We cannot actually say the nature is "unborn," because the notion of something being unborn is still limited by duality. Nor can we simply say that the nature is "empty," because it is not merely "emptiness." In reality, the nature is that which is totally beyond all limited notions of "emptiness." Thoughts of emptiness are deceiving, since as they do not truly describe the nature of reality. Briefly, uncountable absolute truth is beyond anything that can be perceived or counted. This is why it is referred to as *uncountable*.

The great Nagarjuna states that reality is beyond four different concepts: (1) "existing" and (2) "nonexisting," in addition to the concepts of (3) "both existing and non-existing" and (4) "neither existing nor non-existing." So reality is beyond all territory designated by the limits of imagination. Completely transcending all such ideas is known as absolute truth, the authentic nature; all concepts about the nature—true though they may be—still exist in the realm of dualistic conceptions.

If we base our understanding on the concepts we just mentioned, we actually prevent ourselves from discovering the nature as it is—these notions can become obstacles to the pure view. This is what Buddha Shakyamuni taught in the *Prajnaparamita*, as in the famous verses we recite from the *Heart Sutra*: "Form is emptiness, emptiness is form. Form is none other than emptiness, emptiness is none other than form." These verses free us from all duality, grasping, and holding, ushering us into the realization of uncountable absolute truth.

Yet why does Svatantrika Madhyamaka label countable absolute truth as "absolute" if it is still limited by conceptions? In his *Madhyamakalankara*, Shantarakshita explains that "Countable absolute truth is very close to the reality of absolute truth, so practitioners can use it to reliably proceed along the path. For this reason, we teachers named it 'countable absolute truth.'" But the division between countable and uncountable absolute truth does not merely exist on the external level: When we practice with the understanding of Svatantrika Madhyamaka, we acquire a personal, direct realization of the nature as it is. Hence, despite the limitations of dualistic conception, it is important to first develop a notion of emptiness, of non-existing. Based upon this notion we are eventually able to move beyond duality. That is, we approach realization of the nature by cultivating a correct understanding of the way phenomena appear on the conceptual level of ordinary human beings.

The different Madhyamaka schools understand uncountable truth in the same way. Accordingly, there is no difference between the Prasangika and Svatantrika Madhyamaka schools in terms of this designation. For this reason, again, Shantarakshita clearly states that there is no birth and no non-birth; no permanence and no impermanence; no existence and no nonexistence. Absolute truth has no names and no labels—it completely transcends all categories. We have now completed our discussion of the division between the two truths.

Madhyamaka and the Vajrayana

Madhyamaka represents the heart teachings of the Glorious Conqueror, Buddha Shakyamuni. Even Vajrayana practices are based on the Madhyamaka view. For example, at the beginning of deity practice we rest in awareness of the true nature, the samadhi of suchness, or *tattva-samadhi*. This meditation on the true nature is none other than meditation on Madhyamaka. It is also known as Dzogchen meditation. The Dzogchen teachings are actually based upon the Madhyamaka teachings. So, even in the practice of Vajrayana, when visualizing the deity we must have the realization of Madhyamaka. When we reach the completion stage known as the "completion stage beyond all characteristics," we are also meditating on Madhyamaka, which is none other than Dzogchen meditation. Basically, the emptiness aspect of the nature is no different regardless of whether one is practicing Madhyamaka or Dzogchen; both involve meditating on the "observant state," or uncontrived, nondual awareness of the true nature.

If this is true, what is the real difference between the way Madhyamaka and Dzogchen introduce practitioners to the true nature? Dzogchen directly approaches the true nature without the use of logic or reasoning. It is a simple way of directly introducing a practitioner to her own awareness, thereby leading to the discovery of her own innate nature. In contrast, Madhyamaka introduces emptiness, or the true nature, by means of logic and reasoning. It is a more investigative, scholarly way of analyzing reality in order to establish the authentic realization of the true nature. This is the technical difference. However, when it comes to the actual nature, it is always the same—there are not two separate natures—regardless of the practice we use to bring forth this realization. You already know this, of course, but we are just reminding you of how important and special these teachings are for all practitioners.

In the Madhyamaka school, all existing phenomena—including

samsara and nirvana—are included within relative and absolute truth. More precisely, all objects of knowledge and realization are embraced by these truths. Relative truth comprises every object of the six senses as well as the sense organs themselves: eye, ear, nose, tongue, body, and mind. The eye object is form, the ear object is sound, the nose object is smell, the tongue object is taste, the body object is feeling or touch, and mental objects are mental projections, thoughts, and conceptions. All functioning agents at the level of subject and object, in addition to the functioning activities themselves, are subsumed in relative truth.

Conversely, absolute truth is the *nature* of the subject's six senses, objects, and functioning activities. Absolute truth is emptiness, the lack of a substantially solid existing self. Within the realm of absolute truth, there is nothing whatsoever to explore aside from the true nature itself, which is a state beyond conception, engagement, and existence. Generally, absolute truth and relative truth are not all that different from one another, since both exist simultaneously and continuously. Consequently, it is often said that there is one nature with two different aspects, or that the nature is beyond all concepts of singularity and plurality. This is how the nature exists.

In the Vajrayana teachings, we always engage in the union of relative and absolute truth. However, this "union" does not mean two distinct, individual ingredients or materials have joined together; instead, it refers to the fact that relative and absolute truth cannot be separated or divided from each other in the first place. Sometimes the Vajrayana refers to this as "the great union." And so the great union is not based upon the mere conceptions of "relative" and "absolute" that are rooted in dualistic perception.

This original, indivisible union is symbolized in the creation stage of certain Vajrayana practices, during which a practitioner visualizes a male and female deity in union.[19] On the level of ordinary dualistic conceptions, these are two separate individuals in blissful embrace. In truth, however, such practice will usher us into the discovery of the natural state where there is no separation. What the deities actually symbolize is the union of skillful means and wisdom, or the union of appearance and emptiness. Thus the Vajrayana teachings speak of the "union of dharmadhatu and wisdom." Since space and wisdom are inseparable, everything is actually in the indivisible state of union. Everything we perceive, see, or think—including ourselves—has the authentic nature of this state. Without such a union, we would not perceive anything at all, because seeing, hearing, and thinking are all dependent upon the natural state that is the union of relative and absolute truth. This understanding of the nature is not limited to the Vajrayana teachings alone, but to the Outer and Inner Tantras as well, including Mahayoga, Anuyoga, and Atiyoga. For all these reasons, the way Madhyamaka understands the two truths is fundamental to all the teachings of the Buddha, particularly to the Mahayana and Vajrayana teachings.

Absence of a Singular and Plural Self-Existing Nature

As we discussed in the beginning of this shedra, the great Longchen Rabjam taught that absolute truth cannot ultimately be realized through reason and logic alone. This being the case, he divided absolute truth in two ways: absolute truth that can be established through logic and reason, and absolute truth that cannot be established through logic and reason. Perhaps I am now translating these terms in a slightly different way, but these are his two basic divisions of absolute truth: countable and uncountable absolute truth. Today we will move on to discuss the aspect of countable absolute truth known as "characteristics." The characteristics of countable absolute truth are further subdivided into two categories: (1) the absence of self-nature and (2) certainty based upon logic and reason.

First, what is the main characteristic of countable absolute truth? Its main characteristic is that is has no self-nature. But what makes this true? It is true because all objects truly lack an inherent, self-existing nature; so the nature that is actually *no nature* should be understood as truth. This was established with logical reasoning by all the ancient Svatantrika Masters, particularly Shantarakshita in the beginning of the *Madhyamakalankara*. He taught the absence of a single self-nature in addition to the absence of a plural self-nature. Oftentimes our dualistic notions lead us to believe that there is either a single, permanently existing thing, or many permanently existing things; these notions are pervasive among Buddhists and non-Buddhists alike. But, by using logic and reasoning instead of guessing, we discover that there is no such permanent self-nature. This so-called "permanent" self-nature only exists in our imagination. These deluded notions are none other than grasping and clinging, since there is neither a single truly existent thing nor plural truly existent things.

To counter the mistaken belief in a substantial self-nature, Shantarakshita and other great masters used logic and reason to establish the authentic view. These reasonings are not limited to mere refutations or arguments against the views of others. In truth, they are means through which anyone can examine reality using sharp intelligence and inner wisdom. We are not talking about believing in some notion and grasping to it, nor are we talking about clinging to any particular view. Rather, we are using penetrating wisdom and intelligence to explore the nature through reason, which has nothing to do with the extremes of belief and non-belief.

Refuting Singularity

I think many of you have Shantarakshita's *Madhyamakalankara*. In the beginning of his treatise, he says, "Whatever the beliefs of our Buddhist school and other non-Buddhist schools, things are not truly self-existent, because they exist neither as a single thing nor as many things." He continued by logically establishing that phenomena do not exist in either of these ways. If this is true, how do phenomena really exist? Shantarakshita explains that phenomena are like mere reflections and mental images; they have no substantial, solid existence at the singular or plural levels. *Nothing* is substantially existent: not singular entities nor plural entities.

When we begin to investigate the truth of this statement, it is helpful to question the identity of the one who perceives things as either singular or plural. We should ask ourselves, "Who is this 'I'?" Generally, most living beings cling to the concept that they exist as a substantial, single entity. So, first we should recognize that we usually believe "I am one." Nobody thinks of him or herself as plural, thinking, "I am three" or "I am five." This notion doesn't even arise. The thought of existing as a single entity is very strong—it is part of deep habit patterns ingrained in the consciousness of every living being.

The thought of being a single, substantial entity is a false notion, a fundamental and mistaken habit pattern. Along with this belief in oneself comes the clinging to one's possessions, such as, "These are my belongings. This is my car. That is my hat..." The clinging to possessions as single, substantial entities is very singular and private, built upon the notion that oneself is substantially solid. Furthermore, it reinforces the habit pattern of perceiving objects as separate and isolated. All the actions that proceed from such a belief—despite the fact that we perform many activities—are attempts to reinforce this state, bringing it back to the "one." Briefly, this fundamental concept shared by all living beings, reflected in our thoughts and actions, leads us to continually attempt to create a singular oneness to ourselves.

As an extension of this process, we conceive of different doctrines, philosophies, and beliefs in which this sense of "oneness" becomes more sophisticated, taking the form of "one principle," "one creator," "one god," or "one uncompounded nature." This happens even in Buddhism, because such ideas are comforting to the habitual patterning of our consciousness and so are readily accepted. We impute many conceptual layers and labels on phenomena and use reason to support our beliefs, projecting a wholeness onto them. The habit patterns of human consciousness grasp to phenomena as substantial; this is how sophisticated beliefs related to our false sense of singularity develop. Since they are comfortable and easy, these notions of sigularity seem to bring some kind of solution to our discomfort. On the other hand, if we release everything, we lose that feeling of comfort and security. And so we want to believe in and cling to our concepts of "oneness."

Generally speaking, many non-Buddhist schools have established fundamental doctrines based on the notion of singularity. Even the Vaibashikas and Sautrantikas of Hinayana Buddhism believe that a single, partless atom is the cause of all things. They never talk about two partless atoms; rather, they hold that the more subtle state of existence is the single, partless atom, held to be the cause of everything. Similarly, although the Mind Only school is more sophisticated, it proposes that self-awareness, free from all taints and duality, is the source of all things. Consequently, even the Mind Only school holds on to a single thing as the basis of existence. So the belief in a singular thing—this thought of "one"—runs deeply in the consciousness of both Buddhist and non-Buddhist schools. The Madhyamaka schools themselves teach the "union of the two truths," which is still a subtle form of grasping to the idea of the two truths as one.

The great masters of Svatantrika Madhyamaka, such as Shantarakshita, refute this idea of singularity since it is an obstacle to beholding the absolute, panoramic view of the nature as it is. Thus every habit pattern of holding and grasping is still within the realm of duality and is still unnatural. Essentially, Shantarakshita teaches us that all Buddhist and non-Buddhist views based upon the idea of either singularity or plurality are false because they are rooted in duality. The true nature is completely free of subject and object.

Refuting Plurality

This is the meaning of the first verse of Shantarakshita's *Madhyamaka-*

lankara. The rest of his treatise uses various reasons to establish why a singular thing cannot exist. And since nothing singular can exist, it is impossible for anything plural to exist; because plurality is comprised of many individual, single things that do not truly exist, nothing can exist collectively, either. In addition, the numbers two, three, four, etc., are completely dependent upon the idea of one, which is an illusion. Consequently, Shantarakshita reasons that nothing exists plurally.

It is important to contextualize Shantarakshita's famous statement that nothing singular or plural exists. On what level is he speaking? He is speaking in terms of absolute truth—his statement does not apply to conventional reality. That is, when Shantarakshita and other great masters of the Svatantrika Madhyamaka school describe absolute reality, there is no such thing as "singular" or "plural." However, they are not making any claims as to whether things exist as singular or plural on the *relative* level. Thus the Svatantrika masters are indirectly accepting that things do indeed exist as singular and plural entities on the relative level.

How Do Phenomena Really Exist?

If the great Svatantrika masters, including Shantarakshita, accept the relative existence of singular and plural entities, in what manner do these relative phenomena really exist? It is said that objects exist in the same way mirages and mental images exist: they are insubstantial, mere appearances. Relative objects exist only to the extent that they are not subjected to penetrating investigation and analysis that would reveal their insubstantial and interdependent nature. For this reason the Svatantrika masters use the metaphors of "mirages" and "mental images" to describe how relative phenomena appear to exist as singular or plural.

Earlier we saw the four characteristics of relative phenomena according to the Svatantrika Madhyamaka school. Shantarakshita and his teacher Jnanagarbha (Yeshe Nyingpo) have their own special way of describing these same characteristics, which can be found in the

Madhyamakalankara. Condensing two of the previous points into one, they use three categories to encompass relative truth. (1) First, they use the Tibetan word *matak* [*ma brta gcig pu nyams dga' ba*] to indicate that relative things appear to be substantially existent only as long as they are not closely investigated or analyzed. Not recognizing their insubstantial nature, beings often perceive phenomena to be very pleasing and satisfying. (2) Second, whatever is born will also die. This implies that phenomena are capable of bringing forth additional phenomena that share similar characteristics. (3) Third, phenomena function according to their appearance and capacity.

This being the case, we should not assume that Shantarakshita and the other Svatantrika masters are refuting relative phenomena when they say, "Things exist neither as singular nor plural entities." They are actually debating the absolute nature. In the *Madhyamakalankara*, Shantarakshita continues by explaining that the One Thus Gone taught that phenomena are unborn and unceasing, utterly beyond the concepts of existence and nonexistence. This is a teaching on absolute truth, where all notions of singularity and plurality are inapplicable.

Further Characteristics of Absolute and Relative Truth

Absolute truth which can be established through logic and reason lacks a self-existing, actual nature. It has no self-nature. In terms of relative truth, when we investigate relative phenomena, there is nothing whatsoever to find. This is the primary characteristic of relative truth. Even though relative phenomena possess the three characteristics we just mentioned—they seem substantial and pleasing, exhibit birth and death, and function—when we really analyze them, we don't find anything tangible. It is like chasing a rainbow; although the rainbow vividly appears, the further you chase, investigate, and analyze it, the more you discover that there is nothing substantial to be found.

In contrast, the characteristic of countable absolute truth is that we *will* find some kind of answer upon investigating it with logic and reason. For instance, we will arrive at conclusions such as "it is beyond conception" or "it is emptiness." And so, absolute truth is emptiness, beyond conception. Unlike relative truth, our minds can find and mentally hold on to logical conclusions about the absolute nature, which is the defining characteristic of countable absolute truth; it yields distinct conclusions when analyzed with logic and reasoning.

On the ultimate level, absolute truth is great emptiness. This is the meditation of Madhyamaka practitioners. Madhyamaka is referred to as the "Middle Way" because emptiness transcends all concepts of existence or nonexistence , of both, and of neither. It is the center. But, as we have already explained, this "middle" does not refer to the center of something with limited boundaries or some kind of tangible edge. Since there is no territory involved, there is also no real center. Hence, the Middle Way is totally beyond duality.

According to the Yogachara Madhyamaka school of Shantarakshita, relative truth originates with mind. All perceptions, conceptions, and other relative phenomena begin in the mind, yet mind itself is emptiness. In a way, relative truth is none other than our thoughts and mental images. But where does mind exist? When we look to the mind, we don't find anything at all. Beholding this state, free from speech and concepts, is absolute truth.

The Five Essential Points of Yogachara Madhyamaka

In his commentary on the *Madhyamakalankara*, Mipham Rinpoche lists the five essential points of Shantarakshita's teachings on Yogachara Madhyamaka.

1. Functionality

The first essential point is that all relative phenomena function perfectly, in accordance with their appearance. As you know, Shantarakshita does not deny or refute relative truth. Due to this quality of functionality, it is possible to find relative phenomena, which carry out different kinds of relative duties. However, phenomena should be perceived as magical displays or the dream-like reflections of mental images.[20] Clinging to objects that appear to the six senses, most beings perceive relative phenomena as solid and substantially existent, despite their complete lack of a substantial nature. Once more, all phenomena are like magical appearances and mental projections. To summarize, the first essential point of Shantarakshita's teachings is that relative phenomena function according to their appearance and carry out specific duties on the relative level.

2. Independent Self-Awareness

The second essential point of Shantarakshita's teaching is that independent self-awareness (Tib. *rang rig*; Skt. *sva-samvedana*) functions on the relative level. Since the functioning of phenomena has its basis in the mind and mental activities, we might ask, "Who is actually experiencing these phenomena?" It is self awareness that experiences relative truth, and beings perceive phenomenal appearances according to their mental habit patterns. Thus Shantarakshita does not refute the ordinary perception of beings—he acknowledges that everyone experiences relative truth according to their conditioning. For example, if an individual perceives phenomena as pleasant, he or she will be happy; if an individual perceives phenomena as disturbing or unpleasant, he or she will become upset. This happiness and suffering are true on the relative level: Nobody has be to asked to perceive phenomena in this way, since the perceptions of beings is always rooted in independent self awareness.

3. Interiority—Phenomena as Mental Projections

The third essential point of Shantarakshita's teaching is the interiority of relative phenomena. According to the Yogachara Madhyamaka school, relative objects do not arise independently, outside of the mind which perceives them. Instead, everything takes place internally within mind itself; relative reality exists within an individual's own experience. But how does this happen? Consciousness projects itself as an external activity (or phenomena) that is reflected back to consciousness itself, at which point the individual begins to analyze and conceptualize this appearance as a seemingly external experience. It is not as though someone else is directing, manipulating, or imputing these appearances onto our consciousness, since they are merely self-reflections of our own minds.

4. Countable and Uncountable Absolute Truth

The fourth essential point of Shantarakshita's teaching is the two-fold division of absolute truth we discussed earlier: countable absolute truth [*rnam grangs pa'i don dom*] that is verifiable through logic and reasoning, and uncountable absolute truth [*rnam grangs ma yin pa'i don dam*] that is not verifiable through logic and reasoning. We could also refer to these divisions respectively as (1) truth closely connected with absolute reality and (2) absolute truth itself.

Regardless of the Buddhist school to which a practitioner belongs, one's initial understanding of absolute truth is limited to countable absolute truth rather than uncountable absolute truth. This is true even for beginning practitioners of Dzogchen, Mahamudra, and Chod. Of course, our ultimate goal is realization of uncountable absolute truth, but at the present time we only have an intellectual understanding of emptiness. We all have the capability of realizing absolute truth, but we begin with a conceptual understanding of the true nature. Nonetheless, understanding countable absolute truth is a very special way of establishing a basis for our realization of uncountable absolute truth.

Svatantrika Madhyamaka masters use a special technique to usher practitioners into the realization of uncountable absolute truth. Because we have such a strong tendency to grasp and cling to phenomena as substantially existent, the Svatantrikas begin by emphasizing a correct understanding countable absolute truth. This is very important for most beginners, since we are born with the innate habit of grasping to existence that has developed over countless lifetimes. So emphasizing a correct understanding of emptiness is a crucial method for immediately reversing our mistaken conceptions of intrinsic existence. Accordingly, we should begin our practice by contemplating the insubstantiality and lack of self-existence of phenomena.

Again, contemplating emptiness is a direct antidote for grasping and clinging to relative truth as substantial, so it is very practical and beneficial for beginning practitioners to cultivate an understanding of uncountable absolute truth. Although we may have received teachings on Dzogchen and Mahamudra, immediately arriving at the state beyond conception is very difficult. Recognizing the limited capabilities of beings, Shantarakshita and other Svatantrika Madhyamaka masters used terminology that can be understood by individuals at different levels of development: They begin with preschool vocabularly and move up through kindergarten, elementary school, high school and college-level terms. For the Svatantrikas, it doesn't make sense to immediately teach beginners from the college level, without first building a strong foundation in the other levels as well.

Buddha Shakyamuni always taught his disciples to meditate on emptiness. This emptiness meditation, corresponding to countable absolute truth, is the first antidote for grasping at phenomena as solid and self-existent. Having thus created a strong foundation in emptiness meditation, practitioners naturally arrive at an understanding of the "emptiness of emptiness," or uncountable absolute truth. Therefore, the two divisions of absolute truth made by the Svatantrika Madhyamaka school is very practical. Mipham Rinpoche explains that this distinction is one of the very special aspects of Shantarakshita's Madhyamaka teachings.

5. Gradual Approach to Uncountable Absolute Truth

The fifth essential point of Shantarakshita's *Madhyamakalankara* is related with uncountable absolute truth. Once more, Shantarakshita does not immediately present us with uncountable absolute truth; instead, he gradually leads us through successively higher stages until we arrive at ultimate truth. Likewise, in his *Essence of Madhyamaka*, Acharya Bhavya states that one must climb the staircase of relative truth in order to arrive at ultimate truth. Countable absolute truth is part of this staircase that leads to uncountable absolute truth. Shantarakshita's teacher Yeshe Nyingpo and his student Kamalashila said the same thing. Yet another disciple of Shantarakshita, Haribhadra, wrote a famous commentary on Maitreya and Asanga's *Abhisamayalankara*, in which he taught the gradual progression from uncountable to countable absolute truth.

Although the division between countable and uncountable absolute truth is mainly associated with the philosophical teachings of Svatantrika Madhyamaka, almost every great master of Tibetan Buddhism—including those belonging to the Prasangika Madhyamaka school—teach according to this divisios. It makes a great deal of sense to teach in this way since this is how realization develops: one gains an understanding of countable absolute truth before achieving realization of uncountable absolute truth. For this reason, countable absolute truth is not a detour from the true nature. Understanding emptiness at the level of conception helps establish the capacity to recognize absolute truth.

Je Tsongkhapa also taught that one must meditate one-pointedly and vigilantly on the nonexistence of ego in order to defeat the long-standing habit of ego-clinging, or clinging to the self. In his famous commentary on Chandrakirti's *Madhyamakavatara*, for example, Tsongkhapa explained that we should not immediately release all conceptions; initially, we should strongly hold on to the conception that no ego exists in order to defeat our deep habit of ego-clinging.

Similarly, the very famous Sakya master known as Gorampa—who was one of the most renowned logicians of Tibetan Buddhism—taught that the majority of beginning practitioners will not immediately realize the true nature, which is beyond the four extremes of existence, nonexistence, both, and neither. Consequently, Goramba taught them to meditate on nonexistence in order to cut through their heavy attachment to existence. By progressively defeating the four extreme views, a practitioner eventually realizes the sky-like nature of the truth as it is. This is similar to moving from an understanding of countable absolute truth to that of uncountable absolute truth.

By now it should be clear that Shantarakshita and the other Madhyamaka masters do not hold countable absolute truth as the final, definitive goal of practice. Countable absolute truth is merely part of a staircase that leads to the recognition of uncountable absolute truth. Shantarakshita asks himself, "If countable absolute truth is not the final absolute truth, why is it called 'absolute truth' at all?" He answers: "Because it is very close to absolute truth—it points to absolute truth which is totally beyond conception." The destination and final goal of practice is to arrive at a complete understanding of uncountable absolute truth. This is why Mipham Rinpoche outlines the five essential points of Shantarakshita's Madhyamaka teachings; his teachings lead to the recognition of uncountable absolute truth. As a final note, it is always important to remember that there is not even a single hair's difference between the Svatantrika and Prasangika views of uncountable absolute truth.

Uncountable Absolute Truth

We have seen how Shantarakshita teaches on countable absolute truth, but how does his *Madhyamakalankara* point out the nature of *uncountable* absolute truth? Speaking from the absolute perspective, Shantarakshita states that since no birth exists, no death exists, either. This means the very notion of cessation has to be released. All habit patterns of grasping to the four extreme views—existence, nonexistence, both, and neither—must be abandoned in order to behold absolute truth. These views simply reflect the way mundane conception perceives reality, and they are deeply rooted in grasping and clinging. Perhaps one holds all four extremist positions, or maybe only one, two, or three. In actuality, there is no such thing as grasping outside of these mundane habit patterns. Consequently, the Supreme One and all the great Buddhist masters taught that we must completely uproot every notion and conceptual anchor based in the habit patterns of grasping and clinging. We have to pull them up one after another. Only then will we discover the panoramic view of the true nature, which is as vast as space.

Svatantrika-Prasangika Distinction: Gradual Versus Instant

Let us briefly return to the differences between Svatantrika and Prasangika Madhyamaka, or *uma rangyupa* [*dbu ma rang rgyud pa*] and *uma tangyurpa* [*dbu ma thal 'gyur pa*]. The principal distinction between the two lies in their respective emphasis on gradual versus instant recognition of uncountable absolute truth. The Svatantrikas focus on a gradual approach to the true nature, whereas the Prasangikas focus on an instantaneous approach to the true nature. As we have just discussed, the Svatantrika school teaches countable absolute truth before moving on to the final view of uncountable absolute truth, using the first as a stepping stone to the second. In a way, the Svatantrikas take a short detour, allowing one's realization to progressively grow before reaching the ultimate view. This is why Svatantrika Madhyamaka uses special terminology and philosophy related with a more gradual approach to understanding the absolute nature as it is.

Assuming a slightly different approach, the Prasangikas immediately jump to uncountable absolute truth, which transcends all reference points and notions of acceptance. They immediately arrive at a definitive understanding of the true nature. With a foundation in this absolute view, Prasangikas use words and philosophy (on the conventional level) to negate the mistaken perceptions of others. Mipham Rinpoche explains that many Tibetan masters have discussed the various differences between Svatantrika and Prasangika, but what really distinguishes them, and the only substantial difference between them, is that one is more gradual while the other is more immediate. In terms of their final goal—arriving at a complete realization of uncountable absolute truth—they are exactly the same. From this perspective, there are no differences between them whatsoever. Mipham Rinpoche comments that neither school contradicts the other, since they are only distinguished by the methods they use to usher students towards the realization of the true nature.

To further elaborate on what we just said, it should be understood that there is no difference between the realization of Svatantrika and Prasangika masters regarding their understanding of the absolute nature; their final goal and realization of wisdom are indistinguishable. Again, only the methods they use to lead practitioners to such understanding are different. The Prasangikas immediately arrive at the center of the nature, without making any distinctions or divisions in terms of approach, and the Svatantrikas first emphasize countable absolute truth as a practical tool to arrive at uncountable absolute truth. Aside from this significant divergence, the Prasangikas and Svatantrikas share the exact same philosophy, views, realization, and understanding of the Buddha's teachings with respect to his teachings on the nature.

The Five Great Reasonings of Madhyamaka

The Madhyamaka schools teach that everything is inseparable from the unborn state of emptiness on the absolute level, using five vajra reasonings to establish this nature. Earlier we mentioned the characteristics of the two truths, and we will continue our discussion by exploring the logic that proves these characteristics. There is no significant difference between the Prasangikas and Svatantrikas in their acceptance of these reasonings; both use the same logical arguments to establish the true nature. This being the case, we must question whether they use these five reasonings in the same way. In fact, they do not. Svatantrika Madhyamaka uses the reasonings to *establish* the absolute nature, while Prasangika Madhyamaka uses the reasonings only to uproot the grasping of others, without asserting anything on the relative level. In other words, Prasangika Madhyamaka does not say, "This applies to relative truth and that applies to absolute truth." Rather, they immediately use the power of logic to instantly uproot and cut through the grasping of others, sweeping them into the recognition of the absolute nature. To summarize: the logic of both schools is the same but the way they apply this logic is different.

The first reasoning is known as the "reasoning of the sharp vajra" or the "reasoning of the sharp wings of vajra logic that eliminates the notion of causes." Second is the "reasoning that eliminates the notion of existence and nonexistence," which invalidates the notion of results. Third is the "reasoning of the four corners that eliminates the notion of both causes and results." Fourth is the "reasoning beyond plural and singular that eliminates all notions about the absolute nature." Finally, fifth is the "great reasoning of interdependent coorigination (dependent arising) that eliminates the notions of all phenomena" and thus establishes emptiness.[21] In general terms, these reasonings uproot grasping to (1) causes, (2) results, (3) both causes and results, (4) the nature, and (5) all notions about phenomena. By way of refuting all notions about phenomena, the fifth reasoning establishes the correct view of emptiness.

What is the purpose of studying all these intellectual concepts and logical arguments? As you know, all the Buddha's teachings are designed to liberate beings from the suffering of cyclic existence; in fact, the whole purpose of the Dharma is to bring beings to the ultimate state of enlightenment. But why is it that we continually suffer and wander in samsara? We suffer due to our grasping and clinging—this is the major cause of our samsaric experiences and our constant wandering in the ocean of suffering. So we must ask ourselves, "Is this grasping part of the nature?" Obviously, all of us know that grasping is *not* part of the true nature of reality, since it is based on perceiving things that are untrue and not even present.

It cannot be said too much—the nature itself is completely beyond grasping and clinging. Therefore, Buddha Shakyamuni taught how to release grasping and clinging in order to help practitioners discover the true nature as it is. He explained that there are two different approaches that lead to a correct understanding and direct experience of this nature: the first technique is the scholarly method of logically investigating reality so as to arrive at intellectual certainty about the nature and thereby release grasping; the second technique is to simply receive pith instructions about the nature of reality and practice according to those instructions. Both are effective methods for removing grasping and its causes.

Regardless of whether one's approach emphasizes scholarly investigation or practice, both methods require meditation, since meditation is the actual, final goal. For that reason, Tibetan Buddhism often uses the terms *che gom* [*dpyad sgom*] and *chok gom* [*chog sgom*] to describe the two different approaches to meditation. *Che gom* refers to meditation that follows a thorough investigation and analysis of reality through logic and reason. After intensely investigating the nature with study, one finally arrives at certainty, relaxes, and meditates according to the view he or she has discovered. In contrast, *chok gom* refers to meditation based on practicing the pith instructions one has received, rather than emphasizing scholarly analysis. In either case, both approaches require meditation practice.

The teachings often warn that if we limit our spiritual path to study, investigation, and analysis, even though we may arrive at a precise intellectual understanding of the teachings, we might become like a parrot! Sometimes a parrot can say many things, but that doesn't mean it knows what it is talking about. Similarly, a deaf person may become a wonderful musician who can play all kinds of beautiful music, but he or she cannot hear the music itself. If we study and contemplate the teachings but fail to engage in meditation, our practice is incomplete and we will not absorb the true meaning of the teachings into our hearts. Study, contemplation, *and* meditation must be practiced in unison.

All the Nyingma and Kagyu masters explain that the purpose of studying and receiving the teachings is to fully absorb them into our hearts. We are not here to collect good stories to tell others, to make long lists of teachings we have received, or to learn the teachings so we can explain them to our friends and look intelligent. We are here to benefit ourselves by absorbing the essential meaning of the teachings into our hearts and minds. Only then can we truly benefit others. Hence, the whole purpose of logically investigating the nature of reality through analysis and study is to discover—within our own experience—that nothing exists substantially, and that grasping and clinging are unnatural hindrances to our joy, peace, realization, and eventual enlightenment. The fruit of practice, or perfect enlightenment, will give us the unlimited ability to benefit countless beings. Put otherwise, once we have achieved some degree of intellectual certainty about the nature, we have to settle down and practice meditation. This is the purpose and goal of our study of Madhyamaka.

The First Great Reasoning of Madhyamaka

We will now discuss the five great reasonings of Madhyamaka in more detail. The first reasoning is called "*Gyu la chodpa dorje zegmai tentsig*" in Tibetan, or "reasoning of the sharp vajra."[22] *Gyu* means "cause" and *la* means "on" or "to." *Chodpa* means "analyzing." I have translated *dorje zegmai* as "sharp vajra," but it can also refer to "lightning"; *dorje* means "vajra" and *zegmai* means "sharp" or "point." Finally, *tentsig* refers to "reasoning" or "logic." Put together, this statement can be translated as the "reasoning of the sharp vajra that eliminates the notion of causes," or the "reasoning of the sharp vajra that uproots grasping to causes." Again, this *vajra* can alternately be translated as "lightning" or "diamond," indicating a logical argument that destroys or cuts through whatever it touches.

The great Svatantrika masters teach that this reasoning establishes the manner in which phenomena actually exist. On the absolute level, phenomena have no substantial existence whatsoever; they are dependently arisen mere appearances, like reflections in a mirror. As such, phenomena are beyond the four sources or corners of birth. Nagarjuna describes these four corners in the first verses of his *Mula-madhyamaka-prajna*: "Not from self, not from other/Not from both, nor without cause/Things do not arise/At any place, at any time."

What proof do we have that this statement is true? Normally we think causes and conditions are truly existent and give rise to results. Therefore we feel that results, or phenomena, are also truly existent. But Nagarjuna and the other Madhyamaka masters explain that results can only arise from causes in four ways: (1) results arise from themselves, (2) from something other than themselves, (3) from both themselves and something other than themselves, or (4) without cause whatsoever.

1. Results Do Not Arise From Themselves

First, if results arose from themselves, they would be self-producing. What, then, would prevent them from perpetually arising? However, phenomena are not self-producing and do not continually arise. This is why, for instance, golden apples don't grow during every season—summer, spring, winter, and fall. And what would be the purpose of phenomena giving birth to themselves? This would result in endless self-birth, because phenomena would have the power to produce themselves. Additionally, what is the temporal relationship between causes and results? Which comes first? If phenomena arose from themselves, results would be their own causes, and the results themselves would exist long before the causes that gave rise to them. In other words, the "cause" would not really be a cause at all, because it would be preceded by its own result! The terms "birth" and "arising" would be meaningless if results were their own causes, since it would mean results (i.e. phenomena) simply continue without end. Yet this does not always happen. For these reasons and others, it is obvious that results do not give rise to themselves.

2. Results Do Not Arise From Others

Second, we will explore the possibility that results arise from something other than themselves by examining several different questions. What is the relationship between cause and result if they are totally distinct? Does the result come from a permanent other or an impermanent other? Finally, does the result develop instantly or gradually?

Let us assume that results arise from permenant causes other than themselves. We must begin by asking ourselves whether these permanent causes instantly or gradually give rise to results. If permanent causes instantly produced results, cause and result would be indistinguishable because they would exist simultaneously, at the same time. There would be no time for the cause to produce a result! In contrast, by claiming that results gradually develop from permanent causes, one asserts permanent causes to be impermanent, or susceptible to change. And, of course, it makes no sense to say that results are both permanent *and* impermanent; since these two possibilities completely contradict each other, even a dummy wouldn't say this.

One may also claim that results develop from impermanent causes other than themselves. In this case, we must ask whether results develop from impermanent causes in the past, present, or future. It makes no logical sense to say that results arise from causes other than themselves in the past, for the past is gone. Likewise, they cannot develop from distinct, impermanent causes in the future, for the future is not yet born. This leaves the alternative that results develop from distinct, impermanent causes in the present. When we examine the present, we discover that this "present" only exists at the conceptual level; there is no single thing we can call "present," since experience continually moves in a chain of instants, moment after moment. The present is constantly changing, changing, changing. Therefore we cannot logically say that anything resides in the present. If someone claims that results develop from impermanent causes in the present, they are assuming that cause and result exist at the same time, in the same instant. Yet if this was true, there could be no temporal cause-effect relationship between cause and result. The teachings compare this situation to the horns of a yak: How could anyone claim that the right horn *causes* the left horn, or vice versa? Since the horns of a yak arise simultaneously, they cannot share a relationship of cause and effect.

Despite the logical inconsistencies we have just pointed out, some people may continue to claim that results develop from present causes. This being the case, do cause and effect make contact with each other as results arise? To claim that they make contact is logically incoherent, since causes precede results—and if the cause was there before the result, how could it make contact with a result that is not present? In the same way, how could a result make contact with a cause that is not present? On the other hand, to say that cause and result do *not* make contact is also illogical: If cause and result were not in contact, how could we say that such and such cause developed such and such result? With no contact between them, it would make no sense to call something a cause and something else its result.

3. Results Do Not Arise From Self or Other

Third, since we have logically refuted birth from self and from other, we have also refuted birth from both self *and* other; this would be subject to the fallacies of the previous two alternatives.

4. Results Do Not Arise From Nothing Whatsoever

Finally, it makes no sense to claim that results are born from no causes whatsoever, for, if this were the case, flowers could grow in the sky or barley could grow from rice seeds. But everyone knows this does not happen. Phenomena are dependently arisen, appearing due to causes and conditions. If phenomena arose without causes, two different things would occur: first, anything could arise without obstruction at any time, because everything would be a cause for everything else, as in the case of sky flowers. Second, nothing would arise at all and we wouldn't see anything due to the lack of causes and conditions. Obviously relative reality does not function in this way.

The great Svatantrika masters explain that relative truth exists on the surface level but does not stand up to thorough logic, investigation, or analysis. It simply dissolves, as if pursuing a rainbow. So, everything is the same on the relative level; however, this logical does not apply to the relative level. Instead, it points to the *absolute* nature of phenomena. This is why Shantarakshita, the great Madhyamaka texts, and all the Tathagatas taught that phenomena—including both subject and object—are unborn. Absolute truth immediately arrives at the unborn state, without taking any detours. Thus, reality on the absolute level is the true natural state as it is.

General Review

As we continue our discussion of the first great reasoning of Madhyamaka, it is important to restrengthen our beautiful motivation of bodhichitta. Upholding this intention in our hearts, we should think: "I am going to study the profound teachings of *Prajnaparamita* and Madhyamaka in order to lead all living beings to unsurpassable buddhahood. First, studying these teachings I will discover the exact word meaning of Madhyamaka. Second, contemplating this deep meaning I will bring about precise knowledge and understanding of the word meaning itself. Finally, through meditation I will directly experience the truth of the teachings. In this way I will fully actualize the 'three wisdoms' of study, contemplation, and meditation, with the purpose of liberating all sentient beings into the permanent state of enlightenment."

Studying the teachings of Madhyamaka will bring about the realization of emptiness through logic and reason; but this realization does not result from simply believing in particular answers to philosophical questions. The point is not to adopt more *ideas*. Rather, we are going to establish the truth of reality by using our own intelligence and wisdom, bringing forth realization of the nature as it is. The Blessed One taught extensively on the truth of emptiness, and it is this emptiness we are establishing with logic and reason. "Logic" and "reason" are known as *rigpa* [*rig pa*] in Tibetan; however, this is not the same rigpa referred to in Dzogchen. Although their pronunciation is the same, these two terms have different spellings. The rigpa we are discussing is called *nyaya* or *yukti* in Sanskrit. The great Nyingma masters Rongzompa[23] and Mipham Rinpoche both define *rigpa* as the "knowledge and intelligence that understands the nature exactly as it is." In other words, *rigpa* means "understanding an object exactly as it is, without exaggeration or depreciation." Again, we will simply translate this term as "logic" or "reason."

We saw earlier that Buddha Shakyamuni taught a great deal about emptiness in the second and third turnings of the wheel of Dharma. When he did so, the One Thus Gone was not exaggerating or attempting to mislead his followers. Nor was he repeating the words of someone else or asking others to believe him without question. The Buddha taught exactly what he saw: the naked nature as it is. There is no doubt that he taught according to his own direct experience. Buddha never said we would encounter this or that trouble if we didn't believe his teachings on emptiness. In fact, he advised his disciples to use their own intelligence to investigate and analyze the truth of their own experience. Following his advice, the great Madhyamaka masters investigated and analyzed the nature of reality using logic and reason. Great teachers such as Nagarjuna and Asanga carefully studied the Buddha's teachings on logic and reason with great vigor, using these tools to bring forth direct realization of the nature so that we wouldn't have to simply believe in what someone said or limit our spirituality to practicing good conduct merely because others told us to. That is not Buddhism. We should use the tools of logic and reason to usher forth the realization and understanding of emptiness.

By investigating the nature of experience and following in the footsteps of the Awakened Ones and great masters, we will eventually discover that all objects of knowledge—both subject and object—can be divided according to relative and absolute truth. These are also known as illusory truth and absolute truth, respectively. They encompass everything. Yet these two truths were not created by the Buddha—again, he was not trying to trick or mislead us, taking us on some kind of detour. He was describing the nature as it is. Relative and absolute truth are each explored with a different kind of logic: the "logic that understands relative truth exactly as it is" and the "logic that understands absolute truth exactly as it is." Both types of logic will lead to realization of great emptiness.

But it is important to understand that great emptiness is not somewhere else, somewhere outside our own experience. Actually, emptiness is the nature of relative truth itself. As you all know, relative truth (phenomenal appearances) and absolute truth (great emptiness) are completely united and inseparable. Upon developing this realization to perfect understanding, we will transcend all difficulties and troubles, all suffering and sadness. Troubles, difficulties, and sadness all arise from not knowing the nature as it is. This "nature" is empty and free of ego. Relative truth is illusory, impermanent, and egoless. Thus taught the Awakened One, Buddha Shakyamuni. By thoroughly studying the logic of Madhyamaka, we can discover this for ourselves. Uniting study, contemplation, and meditation, we will follow the example of Nagarjuna and Asanga. Many renowned Madhyamaka masters engaged in this kind of practice and thereby achieved the highest realization possible for human consciousness. Such masters are part of the "chains of golden mountains," a term that refers to the realized beings who appeared in India and Tibet. They were totally free from suffering, having reached the state of fearlessness which is totally devoid of worry, sadness, and suffering, based upon their authentic realization of the true nature. Such masters became true heroes and heroines of realization. Maintaining this understanding in our hearts and minds, let us continue the teaching.

Distinctions Between Svatantrika and Prasangika Madhyamaka

Of course, the two major Madhyamaka schools are Svatantrika and Prasangika Madhyamaka. Svatantrika Madhyamaka divides absolute truth in two ways: absolute truth that can be established through logic (countable) and absolute truth that cannot be established through logic (uncountable). Among these two, we are currently discussing the first. This first kind of absolute truth is often expounded according to its characteristics. Again, the characteristics of absolute truth that can be established through logic are themselves divided into (1) "actual characteristics" and (2) "logic that correctly proves the certainty of these characteristics."

The logic that establishes the characteristics of countable absolute truth with certainty uses descriptions we have heard many times. For instance, we chant these words while reciting the *Heart Sutra* and other sadhanas, saying,"Everything is emptiness, unborn, unceasing, and beyond coming and going." Now we must use logic and reason to establish with certainty that such verses authentically describe the nature of absolute truth. That is, we must prove for ourselves that absolute truth is unborn, unceasing, and beyond all conceptual fabrications.

Earlier, we briefly listed the five great reasonings of Madhyamaka that bring about realization by establishing absolute truth as emptiness. These reasonings are called *ten tsig nga*, *rigpa nga*, or *ten nga* in Tibetan. Their Sanskrit equivalents are *panca-nyaya*, *panca-yukti*, *panca-tarka*, and also *panca-hetu*. This Sanskrit *hetu* is *tang* in Tibetan. *Nyaya* and *rigpa* are roughly translated as "intelligent logic," while *hetu* and *tang* can be translated as "sign," "indication," or "reason." Once more, *rigpa* means "logic." Finally, *nga* means "five."

Related with these reasonings is another Tibetan term called *tsema* [*tshad ma*], which means "valid cognition." *Tsema* is a synonym of the Sanskrit term *pramana*. *Pra* means "first" and *mana* means "ascertainment." So *pramana* means "first ascertainment," or the first, undeluded instant of ascertainment or discernment; generally, this moment of perception is considered to be accurate. The following moments of perception, however, may be deluded. Thus *tsema*, or valid cognition, is unmistaken conception or thought.

Any of the five great reasonings of Madhyamaka is enough to bring forth a profound realization of emptiness, serving as a wake-up call to mind that mind itself is empty. Still, the great Madhyamaka masters emphasized these ten tsig nga in slightly different ways. Normally when we examine the objects of knowledge in samsara, we can see that there are (1) causes and (2) results, and (3) both causes and results have some kind of identity or nature. These three terms are known as (1) *gyu* [*rgyu*], *de wu* [*'bras bu*], and *ngo wo* [*ngo bo*] in Tibetan.

Review of the First Great Reasoning of Madhyamaka

The first great reasoning of Madhyamaka—the reasoning of the sharp vajra—is mainly designed to demonstrate the emptiness of causes, using a number of logical arguments. So the first reasoning focuses on the *cause* aspect of knowledge. In terms of conventional reality, everybody knows that causes develop results and that results arise from causes. Buddha taught the emptiness of causes according to the level of *absolute* truth; relatively speaking, causes do exist. As we saw earlier, Shantarakshita's *Madhyamakalankara* explains that relative reality, or illusory truth, has a purpose, since relative phenomena exist conventionally and function in accordance with their appearances. Yet they have no substantial, solid existence on the absolute level. Not investigating or analyzing the nature of illusory phenomena, we experience only temporary pleasure. Nonetheless, relative phenomena have no ultimate existence. For this reason, the different Madhyamaka schools explain that phenomena are unborn: They are not born from themselves, from others, from both, or without cause whatsoever. These reasons all point to the absolute nature of appearances. By discovering that birth does not truly exist, we can release our grasping to birth as substantially solid.

Once more, it is important to emphasize that birth appears to exist on the relative level of illusory truth as long as we don't investigate and analyze the absolute nature of phenomena. Of course things are born! Nobody is arguing that birth does not exist at all. However, when we investigate relative truth, our understanding of phenomena becomes more and more subtle, until phenomena finally disappear altogether—like chasing a rainbow. We have already examined the four different ways that phenomena could be born and logically established that each possibility collapses upon itself. Since there are no other alternatives, we have proven that birth does not exist on the absolute level. So we can relax and settle our minds regarding this issue. This logic applies equally to all phenomena.

When we say there is no birth, we are not just referring to the birth of particular individuals, such as seeds. All objects of knowledge—subjects, objects, consciousness, and objects of consciousness—are unborn. Simply put, samsara and nirvana are unborn. And if there is no birth, there is also no existence. And if there is no existence, what could possibly cease? We read this in many texts, including the teachings of Dzogchen: "Phenomena are free from birth, existence, and cessation." What do we call something that is free from these three characteristics? We call it "great emptiness" or the "great completion stage." But this is just a name that accords with our common conceptions. Great emptiness itself does not exist substantially, yet it is not a weak or blank emptiness. It is not like the religious sects of ancient times that prayed to the sun; they believed the sun was a god and that it was divine. In other words, they placed appearances on one side and emptiness on the other, as if they were two distinct departments. We will avoid this duality by cultivating the vivid realization that emptiness is unborn, and, as we continue to meditate on this, we will discover that "emptiness" is not just a word, a concept, or an intellectual game. We must carefully meditate on the absence of birth, cessation, and existence (residing). As we develop this realization and progress in our practice, it is important to continue our studies. Emptiness is not limited by our brains or intellectual understanding; we must absorb the truth of emptiness into our hearts and meditate on the true nature, continuing the glorious tradition of the great masters of the past.

The Second Great Reasoning of Madhyamaka

The second great reasoning of Madhyamaka is called "*Drebu la chopa yomed che gog gi tentsig*" in Tibetan.[24] *Drebu* means "result" or "fruit," while *la* means "on" or "at." Again, *chodpa* means "analyzing." *Yod* means "existing" and *med(pa)* means "non-existing." *Che gog* refers to "birth" and also "refuting," "stopping," "preventing," and "negation." *Gi* is a grammatical marker indicating possession. Finally, *tentsig* means "reason" or "logic." Altogether, this can be roughly translated as the "reasoning that eliminates or analyzes the notions of existence and nonexistence."

As we just mentioned, any of these reasonings can bring about a realization of emptiness. This time, however, we are mainly focusing on the reasoning that eliminates the notion of results. On the relative level, results are often very similar to their causes, since cause and result are intimately associated with one another. So causes and results are not all that different. When analyzing results, we must ask whether they come from existence, nonexistence, both, or neither (i.e. nothing at all). Another slightly different way of putting it is to ask whether they come from self, other, neither, or nothingness.

It is important to recognize that we are not just talking about one result; in a way, *everything* we see right now is the result of a past causes. Thus the actual object of debate is whether all the phenomena we currently experience exist in the way we perceive them. What we are trying to prove is that these objects do not innately exist on the absolute level; ultimately speaking, phenomena are not really there. Everybody agrees that we are perceiving *something*. The disagreement between ourselves and others is whether these appearances exist as substantial entities or not. We are logically going to establish that, on the absolute level, none of these appearances exist substantially. In Tibetan this is called *drubja* [*bsgrub bya*], our "statement" or "purpose." It is the issue we are going to debate. Others will respond, "Why is that so?," or "What makes you say this?" We will respond to others in the same way.

We have already touched base with the logical reasons put forth by the Madhyamaka schools as to why phenomena do not exist in the absolute sense. First, because phenomena are unborn, they do not come from existence; second, they do not come from nonexistence; third, they do not come from birth; and fourth, they do not come from nothingness. We can rephrase these subvisions to understand them in a slightly different way: first, phenomena do not exist because they are not born from existence; second, nor are they born from nonexistence; third, by refuting the first two possibilities, phenomena cannot logically be born from both; and fourth, phenomena are not born from neither, or nothingness.

1. Phenomena Do Not Arise From Existence

Now we will logically establish the truth of these statements using the reasons put forth by the great Madhyamaka masters. First, if phenomena already existed or pre-existed (in something existent), there would be no need for them to be born, since they would already exist! We have to think about the truth of this statement. If phenomena already existed before they were "born" (i.e. if a plant already existed in a seed), then there would be no need for them to be born again. Even the dictionary's definition of "birth" implies that something arises which was not already present. Additionally, if phenomena pre-existed in other phenomena, they would continually produce duplicates—for if something arose from itself, what would prevent it from continually arising? There are many different logical arguments that establish insubstantiality of phenomena. Essentially, if phenomena—which are results—already existed in their causes, they could not be "born." If this occurred, the word "born" would lose its meaning. Therefore, no results come from existence.

2. Phenomena Do Not Arise From Nonexistence

Second, if results arose from nonexistence, the whole phenomenal world we currently perceive must have arisen from nonexistent causes. We can use a logical argument from the previous reasoning to establish the truth of this statement. How could results, or phenomena, develop from nonexistent causes? They can't. To say that existence comes from nonexistence does not make any logical sense, for if something came from nonexistence—or lack of existence—it would not exist. If there was nothing, or no cause whatsoever, how could results develop from this nothingness? Can we claim that we were born from the horns of a rabbit, which do not exist? We cannot. Similarly, results cannot develop from nonexistent causes.

3. Phenomena Do Not Arise From Both Existence and Nonexistence

Third, neither can we say that results come from both existence *and* nonexistence. The concepts of existence and nonexistence contradict each other; they are opposites. Accordingly, how could results develop from mutually exclusive opposites? If we were to say that something exists, that very statement refutes nonexistence, and so it makes no sense to say that results come from both existence and nonexistence. Such an assertion is subject to the same logical fallacies as the first two alternatives we just discussed. We have just established that results do not arise from existence, nonexistence, or both.

4. Phenomena Do Not Arise From Nothingness

Fourth, results do not arise from neither existence nor nonexistence; stated differently, results do not arise from nothingness. Once again, we must ask ourselves, "How could anything develop from nothingness?" We will use a similar logical argument as in the reasoning of the sharp vajra to refute this alternative. If phenomena arose from nothingness, did they arise long ago in the past, in the present, or in the future? Upon investigating these possibilities, we discover that results could not possibly develop from nothingness in any of the three times. If we were to argue such a position, we would imply that nothingness has divisions; we are making nothing—or no *thing*—into a thing, an object of awareness. For instance, nothingness either changes or is unchanging. If nothingness changes and something develops from it, this implies that "nothingness" is actually something, and that this something changed into something else. On the other hand, if nothingness is unchanging, how could results ever develop from it?

All is Emptiness

By examining these four different possibilities, we have logically established that results, or phenomena, do not arise and are not born on the absolute level. On the illusory level of relative reality, however, phenomena exist and are present. The more we investigate and analyze results, the more we discover that we cannot find any tangible location or essence to phenomena which can be held in the mind. This is known as emptiness. From the absolute perspective of emptiness, all phenomenal appearances are perceived as illusions. This is why the great Svatantrika masters taught that results do not exist on the absolute level; all results are emptiness.

In his *Madhyamakalankara*, Shantarakshita explains that phenomena appear to be true, beautifully performing and functioning on the relative level, as long as we don't thoroughly investigate or analyze them. Hence, it is important to bring about a realization of emptiness to cut through our present dualistic conceptions, which always tend to grasp and hold on to phenomenal appearances. But we don't stop at grasping to phenomena; deep in our consciousness, we think everything is very substantial, indestructible, and impermanent. This perception itself is none other than grasping and clinging. Of course, the Vajrayana is known as the "Indestructibe Yana," but we perceive ourselves as indestructible sentient beings, with indestructible duality and indestructible grasping. We believe in substantiality and singularity on a deep level. How could we possibly believe that such a big mountain is emptiness, that the ocean is emptiness, or that the earth is emptiness? If we said this to others, they would laugh! They would think we have lost our minds! Duality mind is extremely strong and hard. For this reason, in one sutra the Blessed One said, "All the beings in the world may debate me, but I will not debate them; I will repeat whatever they say. If they say it is white, I will say it is white. If they say it is red, I will say it is red. If they say it exists, I will say it exists. Likewise, if they say it does not exist, I will say it does not exist, following their lead." Buddha Shakyamuni taught the provisional meaning of the Dharma according to the capability of beings and was always sensitive to the context.

On the absolute level of great emptiness, there is no birth and no results. There are also no causes: All are emptiness. The reasonings we have just discussed were used by the great Madhyamaka masters to usher forth a vivid realization of absolute truth in the minds of practitioners. Still, it is important to remember that these logical analyses are not just intellectual games. They are part of our meditation practice. Each time we investigate phenomena and discover their insubstantial nature, we should relax completely and absorb this realization into our hearts and minds. This has been our brief discussion of the second great reasoning of Madhyamaka, which eliminates the notion of results.

Nagarjuna, Aryadeva, and the Five Reasonings

Although the five great reasonings of Madhyamaka can be found throughout the teachings of the Buddha, they were compiled by the great Madhyamaka masters. The first great reasoning was taught most famously by Arya Nagarjuna in the first verses of his *Mula-madhyamaka-prajna*. They read: "*Dag le ma yin zhen le min, nyi le ma yin gyu me min, ngopo gang dag gang na yang, chewa nam yang yod ma yin.*" Let us briefly discuss the meaning of these words. *Dag le ma yin zhen le min* means "not from the self and not from others." *Nyi le ma yin gyu me min* is translated as "not from both and not from neither." *Ngopo* means "all this material," "all these substances or things." Then *chewa nam yang yod ma yin* reads, "Since no birth exists, nothing whatsoever has been born."[25] Arya Nagarjuna uses many logical arguments to prove the truth of this statement—which eliminates the notion of causes—throughout his famous *Mula-madhyamaka-prajna*.

The Prasangika and Svatantrika Madhyamaka schools mainly developed based upon differing interpretations of Nagarjuna's four verses by Buddhapalita and Bhavaviveka, respectively. As we discussed at the beginning of this shedra, Buddhapalita is the Sanskrit name of the master whose interpretation of Nagarjuna's verses gave rise to the Prasangika school; he is known as Sangye Khyang [*Sangs rgyas bskyangs*] in Tibetan. Bhavaviveka is the Sanskrit name of the master whose interpretation of Nagarjuna's verses gave rise to the Svatantrika school; his Tibetan name is Lobpon Lobpon Leg Den Je [*slob dpon legs lden 'byed*] in Tibetan. In addition to their renown as great scholars, these two masters were also mahasiddhas. It is said that Buddhapalita achieved enlightenment within his lifetime, and that Acharya Bhavya did not abandon his body towards the end of his life, but simply flew off into the sky.

The second great reasoning of Madhyamaka that eliminates the notion of results also comes from the teachings of the Buddha and the verses of Nagarjuna. However, most Tibetan commentators quote Aryadeva—Nagarjuna's foremost disciple—to support this reasoning. Shantarakshita's principal disciple also quotes Aryadeva in his discussion of the famous reasonings of Madhyamaka. Aryadeva's teaching reads: "*Yodpa chewa rig min te, medpang namkai metok zhin, detar yod dang medpa la, kepa nam yang mi zhin do.*"[26] First, *yodpa chewa* roughly means "birth of something existent is not logical." Second, "Birth of something nonexistent is like a flower in the sky." Third, "Both notions—birth from existence and nonexistence—are illogical." And finally, "Therefore, the wise should not cling to any views."

General Review

Up to this point we have discussed the first two of the five great reasonings of Madhyamaka, beginning our teachings on the third point with quotations from Aryadeva. As we continue our exploration of the profound Madhyamaka teachings, it is important to restrengthen our beautiful motivation of bodhichitta, which is the intention to liberate all living beings into the state of supreme enlightenment. Enlightenment is completely free from duality, conceptualization, and grasping. So let us continue our studies in order to bring all beings to this ultimate realization of the nature.

The teachings of Guru Padmasambhava and the Nyingma school often emphasize the unity of study, contemplation, and meditation. These three should be practiced together, never separated from one another and practiced individually. Consequently, in addition to our study of Madhyamaka, we must deeply contemplate the teachings and meditate on them. By practicing in this way we will avoid extreme views, absorbing the teachings and knowledge we have cultivated into our hearts. Only then will they truly benefit our growth towards the final goal of enlightenment, or complete realization of the true nature.

It is often said that even if we study only one line of the teachings, we should base our study upon the altruistic intention of bodhichitta, never separating our activities from the nutrition of the "mind of enlightenment," as it is called in Tibetan. Bodhichitta is like protein or vitamins that help us grow in the right direction. It is especially important to base our Dharma-related activities—including study, contemplation, and meditation—in the strong foundation of bodhichitta. Love, compassion and wisdom are not strange ingredients or mental states that we find somewhere outside ourselves: Actually, bodhichitta is the authentic nature of mind itself, which has the dual aspects of clarity (i.e. luminosity) and emptiness.

Emptiness and Clarity

The emptiness of mind we have been discussing is not blank emptiness, since it is inseparable from clarity. And clarity is none other love, compassion, and wisdom—bodhichitta itself. When we bring forth, restrengthen, and activate this power in our minds, we naturally become more joyful, appreciative, confident, and understanding. So, bodhichitta is the medicine that dispels ignorance, attachment, and anger. It reveals our innate wisdom and allows us to penetrate all notions related with subject and object, relative and absolute, and they become easy to understand. Having thus taken bodhichitta and the recognition of emptiness as the very essence of practice, our beautiful qualities will shine and grow like the lushness of springtime.

Mind is filled with many beautiful qualities, but at the present time we are overpowered by dualistic tendencies; it is almost as if our positive qualities are hiding or sleeping. By cultivating bodhichitta, these qualities awaken and become known as "wakefulness." This is why Buddha Shakyamuni was known as the "Fully Awakened One"; he completely developed the sleeping, hidden qualities of the nature within himself and thereby achieved perfect enlightenment. Yet we have to motivate this awakening within ourselves, because we have been afflicted by duality mind for so long. We need to develop an understanding of dependent origination, in which our beautiful qualities mutually support one another and lead to understanding and realization of the true nature.

When we investigate the clarity aspect of mind, what do we find? Again, we discover that there isn't anything substantial, solid, or tangible to hold on to. This quality itself is the beauty of the nature. For this reason the Buddha referred to phenomenal appearances as a "magical display." But it is not as though he was trying to use fancy words or please others by talking about magic! The nature truly *is* magical. Even though phenomena are without a substantially, inherently existing core, they are so beautiful, endless and uninterrupted. The clarity of the nature unceasingly sparks forth, transmuting and transforming, emanating and merging, coming and going in a great show of the nature. How beautiful! Within the endless display of appearances, there is nothing whatsoever to grasp or hold.

Grasping spoils the natural radiance of arising phenomena by obscuring the beauty of the nature and leading to many difficulties and troubles. In response to the grasping habit patterns of beings, Nagarjuna and the other great Madhyamaka masters taught in such as way as to introduce us to the beauty of the nature, so that we can simply relax in the openness of mind without clinging to the iceberg of duality as if it were a precious jewel. All that arises is empty, and emptiness continually arises, arises. Such is the nature of everything, the very nature of what Dzogchen—the pinnacle of the Glorious Conqueror's teachings—always points to. The unceasing display of clarity and emptiness is the very nature of mind. When we discover the nature of mind, we begin to discover the nature of everything. In general, this recognition begins in one's own heart and extends out from the center of oneself to others. Thus, mind is referred to as empty *and* luminous; for although the mind is empty, emptiness sparks forth in a radiant, unceasing display of clarity, or the arising clarity of bodhichitta—of love, compassion, and wisdom. These qualities are themselves inseparable from emptiness, so there is no substantially existent love, compassion, or wisdom that we can cling to like a stone. Nothing is substantially solid.

And so, mind is often referred to as the inseparable union of clarity and emptiness. The Supreme Teacher described the nature of mind in many different ways: alternately as the union of appearance and emptiness, the union of great blissfulness and emptiness, and the union of absolute truth and relative truth emptiness. On the level of reality, all arising appearances are the inseparable union of these qualities, which exist in a single, indivisible state. The teachings often compare this union to a fire and its warmth, since one cannot be distinguished from the other. Likewise, emptiness and appearances cannot be separated from each other; they are reflections of a single state, or nature, with two different aspects.

In his *Mula-madhyamaka-prajna*, Nagarjuna compares this situation to molasses and sweetness in addition to fire and its warmth. In the same way, emptiness and appearances are inseparable. The entire phenomenal display—all appearances without exception—are empty. Usually when we say that something is a "union," we imply that two different ingredients have been added together to make a whole. Such is not the case with the nature of reality, which cannot be divided at all, in the same way water and its moisture can only be separated at the level of concepts. The true nature cannot be divided, categorized, or separated. This is the nature of everything!

But if the entire universe and world—including our own minds—are in an indivisible state of union, why do great masters such Nagarjuna and the Buddha himself emphasize emptiness, emptiness, emptiness? Why not appearances? It is because duality mind does not grasp very much to notions of emptiness; rather, it tends to grasp and cling to *appearances*, or objects of perception. Because we are overwhelmed by dualistic conceptions, we tend to hold on to everything we experience, including the places we go and the activities we engage in. So all this talk of emptiness is designed to help us see past the mere surface of appearances and break down our beliefs about substantially existent phenomena.

The True Nature of Appearances

From the absolute perspective, appearances exist on the level of mind and imagination; they do not exist externally in any substantial way. Thus, phenomenal appearances are the display of mind. Although we make divisions between past, present, and future—or east, south, north, andwest—when it comes to mind, all these divisions merge together without distinction. Mind puts them together. For this reason, appearances are known as "imagination" or "display." These mental conceptions are the same as external objects, in the sense that they have no substantiality and cannot be found upon looking. Although we give different names to objects, all phenomenal appearances and divisions come together in mind—everything is mixed up in a single state. Nothing exists in any solid way, since it is mind itself that imputes substantiality upon phenomena.

All this means external objects do not exist as we ordinarily perceive them. They are completely empty of solid existence. Likewise, mental images, imagination, and appearances are emptiness. So the Madhyamaka teachings often state, "External objects and inner objects are all inseparable from the state of great emptiness." The gracious and wise teacher, Buddha Shakyamuni, repeatedly said, "All phenomena are without identity and name." As we have discussed throughout this shedra, phenomenal existence has no substantiality whatsoever; it is empty and without self-nature.

Names, too, are without substantial existence: They are mere labels attributed to objects, and therefore are totally created by mind. As such, there is no true relationship between names and objects, as we simply refer to objects based upon our own mental conceptions. Nagarjuna said, "Names and objects have no real relationship. It would often be dangerous if names and objects had a strong relationship!" For example, if names and their objects were the same, saying the word "fire" would burn our mouths! A name is just a name, and fire can be referred to by many different words precisely because names and objects are distinct. Names do not exist substantially in the way that earth, for instance, exists on the relative level. This is why the word "earth" is not identical to the earth element—the word "earth" is created by imagination, by mind. Most of the Buddhist schools, from Sautrantika to Vajrayana, teach that names are just imagination: they are ideas, nominatives, illusions, and mind.

The Third Great Reasoning of Madhyamaka

The third great reasoning of Madhyamaka is known as "*Gyu dre nyika la chopa muzhi che gog gi tentsig*" in Tibetan.[27] *Gyu dre* means "cause and result." *Nyi* means "both" and *la* means "to" or "at." *Chodpa* means "analyzing," and *mu zhi* means "four corners." *Che* means "birth" and *gog* means "negation," "stopping," or "preventing." Finally, *tentsig* means "reason" or "logic." We have already discussed most of these words in the previous two sections. This entire statement can be roughly translated as the "reasoning that analyzes and eliminates the four corners of the birth of causes and results," or the "reasoning of the four corners that eliminates the notions of both causes and results." In terms of pronunciation, this *chodpa* is the same sound used in the term *Trekcho*, referring to the Dzogchen practice of "cutting thoroughly," in addition to the term *Chod*, referring to the "cutting through" technique practiced by Padampa Sangye and Machig Labdron. However, this *chodpa* is transliterated as *dpyod pa*.

In its analysis of causes and results, the third reasoning of Madhyamaka establishes that both causes and results are emptiness. The subject of debate is the following: Are all appearances—all phenomenal existence—the results of past causes? Will these appearances themselves be the causes of future results? Is everything we now see both a cause and result? According to the Madhyamaka tradition of Shantarakshita, phenomena do not exist on the absolute level.[28] They they simply do not exist as we ordinarily perceive them. The reason *why* phenomenal appearances do not exist substantially on the relative level is because they are "free from one and free from many." That is, phenomena neither exist as singular entities nor as plural entities.

Relationship Between Causes and Results

As we explained earlier, Shantarakshita's teacher was the great master Jnanagarbha (Tib. Yeshe Nyingpo), who wrote a famous book entitled *Uma Den Nyi* [*dBu ma bden gnyis*], or *Division of the Two Truths*. In this work, Jnanagarbha analyzes the following four propositions: (1) that many causes develop one result; (2) that one cause develops many results; (3) that many causes develop many results; and (4) that one cause develops one result. His work logically establishes that, on the absolute level, there are no causes, no results, and no birth.

In his renowned work on the two truths, Jnanagarbha offers a famous quotation that analyzes the four propositions we just mentioned. The first line is "*Dumay chig gi ngo mi je*" [*dbu mas gcig gi dngos mi byed*] in Tibetan. *Dumay* means "many," while *ngowo* means "nature" and *chig* means "one." *Mi* means "not" and *je* means "perform." So the word meaning of the first line is, "Many will not perform one." Our translation of this line is "Many causes will not develop one result." The second line is "*Chig gi dumai ngo mi je*" [*gcig gis du ma'i dngos mi byed*]. Again, *chig* is "one" and *gi* is "by." *Duma* means "many" and *ngo* means "substance" or "things." *Mi* is a negation and *je* means "perform." Thus, "One cause will not develop many results." The third line is "*Dumay duma je ma yin*" [*du mas du ma byed ma yin*]. The word meaning of this statement is "by many to many." However, the true meaning of this statement is, "Many causes will not bring many results." Finally, the fourth line is "*Chig gi chig je pa yang min*" [*gcig gis gcig byed pa yang min*], which means, "One cause will not develop even one result."[29] This quotation explains that birth, causes, and results do not exist on the absolute level—all is emptiness.

As we have discussed throughout this shedra, Svatantrika Madhyamaka makes the distinction between relative and absolute truths. On the relative level, we all know that causes develop results. But what Jnanagarbha is investigating is the exact relationship between these causes and results. Let us now consider his first proposition—that many causes develop one result. Obviously, nobody believes that many causes bring about a single result, since this contradicts our shared experience of conventional reality. Such a thing does not exist. For instance, if we plant many different kinds of seeds, they will not all produce a single piece of corn. The second possibility—that one cause develops many results—is similar to the first, in that it is not based on valid reasoning. It is impossible. Again, planting one seed of barley will not produce an entire field of plants. Likewise, many causes cannot develop many results, nor can one cause develop many results. Just as a single cause does not itself produce a building, one cause cannot produce many buildings. Although many causes come together to make the building, in the end only one building remains. So, causes and conditions produce results only on the relative level. From the absolute perspective, this cause-result relationship does not exist in the way we normally perceive it.

Do Cause and Result Occur Simultaneously?

Furthermore, do causes and results occur simultaneously or at different times? As in our discussion of the reasoning of the sharp vajra, if results and their causes occurred at the same time, there would be no point for the results to develop at all; the result would already be present with the cause. But if causes and results occurred at the same time, what would be the difference between them? Having developed simultaneously, they could not share a relationship of cause and result (effect).

Do Cause and Result Make Contact?

Again, we must ask whether cause and result make contact with each other. If they *do* make contact, by the same logic we used before cause and result must be identical, having developed in the same place at the same time. It then becomes meaningless to call one a "cause" and the other its "result." On the other hand, if cause and result are *not* in contact with one another when the result develops, how can we say the result comes from the cause? All these reasons point to the insubstantiality of causes and results, which have no solid, concrete existence. Instead, causes and results are like magically-arisen magical displays. When we investigate the relationship between causes and results, we cannot find a satisfactory answer.

From the absolute perspective, there is no substantial existence to be found. But even though we use the word "emptiness" to describe phenomenal appearances, it does not mean we are ignoring relative truth. The Svatantrika Madhyamaka school accepts everything on the relative level, seeing causes and results as a function of conventional reality. Still, although the Svatantrikas put forward and debate the relative functioning of phenomena, they also teach that phenomena do not exist as we perceive them on the absolute level. It cannot be emphasized enough: Svatantrika Madhyamaka never claims that phenomena do not exist on the level of conventional reality.

The Fourth Great Reasoning of Madhyamaka

The fourth great reasoning of Madhyamaka is called "*Ngowo la chopa chig duma drel gyi tentsig*" in Tibetan.[30] *Ngowo* means "nature" and *chodpa* means "analyzation." *Chig* means "one" and *duma* means "many." Again, *tentsig* means "reason." So this statement can be roughly translated as the "reasoning that analyzes the nature which is free from both one and many," or the "reasoning beyond plural and singular that eliminates all notions about the absolute nature."

At the beginning of his *Madhyamakalankara*, Shantarakshita writes, "Regardless of what Buddhist and non-Buddhist schools say about existing phenomena, phenomena do not really exist on the absolute level." He continues by reasoning that phenomena do not exist as either singular or plural entities. If phenomena truly existed, however, they would have to exist in singular or plural form. Therefore, the phenomenal appearances we see are like mere reflections from a mirror.

We briefly discussed this point earlier in our shedra. Ordinarily, duality mind grasps to the notion of "oneness," which is a habit pattern deeply ingrained in the consciousness—or alaya—of every living being. This notion is extremely strong. All of us tend to believe that the universe is "one," and we think of ourselves as individuals. This sense of oneness is powerfully felt by almost every sentient being. The same goes for our ego-clinging. Our ego is "one." Thus we believe that the universe is one, the ego is one, and "I" am one." Briefly, those who follow different religions have the thought of "one," and those who don't follow any religion at all *also* believe in this "one" very strongly. Shantarakshita is refuting this notino of oneness.

We can begin our refutation of entities as singular and plural by stating that singularities do not exist even on the material level. The body, for example, is not just a single, solid object; instead, it is a combination of many different ingredients, objects, and things. The teachings of the Buddha describe the body as having over 360 principal bones as well as various different organs, channels, and nerve systems. Each one of these things is a part of the body, which is a combination of many heaps of objsects all put together. For this reason, Shantarakshita explains that phenomena do not exist as singular entities; there are no singular things, just heaps of many different things.

The Great Preceptor continues by explaining that certain Buddhist schools also believe in singularity, including the Vaibashikas and Sautrantikas who hold "partless atoms" to be the cause of all mass, matter, and objects. Furthermore, they claim that one "partless instant" is the cause of all time. Generally speaking, Buddhists often speak of "one consciousness" free from duality. In other words, the different schools of Buddhism also maintain this notion of oneness. On the absolute level no partless atoms, no partless instants, and no awareness free from duality actually exist!

Many non-Buddhist philosophical schools believe in one soul, one time, or one principal. But as you know, this oneness has no substantial existence on the absolute level. We should begin by thoroughly investigating our notions of singularity and searching for their location, asking ourselves, "Where is this "one?" By analyzing our beliefs in singularity with logic and reason, we will discover that nothing has any substantial, solid existence; our notions of oneness are purely imaginary. Everything is emptiness.

Seeing as how we have refuted the notion of a substantially existent "one," how could many objects develop from this nonexistent singularity? As we discussed earlier, all notions of many begin with one, and the very concept of "many" is based upon multiple singularities put together. Because we have eliminated the notion of single entities, it is logically impossible for plural entities to exist, either. The great teacher Vasubandhu often said "plurality is just another illusion." Once more, the word "plural" is a name for many singular entities joined together, as in a garland of beads or an army of people. But when we take away the notion of beads and people themselves, the collective garlands and armies no longer exist. They are seen to be unsubstantial illusions. Without one there cannot be many.

This is the absolute side of the nature. On the relative level, singular and plural obviously exist. Shantarakshita is not refuting relative phenomena, nor is he saying that we cannot name or label conventional reality. He is simply explaining that, on the absolute level, phenomena are not really there. They are conceptions and imagination.

Shantarakshita begins his *Madhyamakalankara* with four lines, the first of which is, "*Dag dang zhen me ngo di dag.*" *Dag* means "ourselves," whereas *dang* means "and" and *zhen* means "other." *Me* refers to "speaking" and *ngo* refers to "things." Hence we could translate the first line as, "These things of which we Buddhists and non-Buddhists speak." Second, "*Yang dag du ne chigpa dang.*" *Chigpa* means "single" and *dang* means "and." Third, "*Dumai rangzhin drelwai chir.*" *Dumai* means "plural" and *rangzhin* means "nature." *Drel* is "freed" and *chir* is "therefore." Finally, the fourth line is, "*Rangzhin me de zugnyan zhin. Rangzhin* is "nature." *Med* is a negation particle and *zugnyan* means "mirror image." *Zhin* means "similar." Together these lines can be translated as, "These things of which we Buddhists and non-Buddhists speak, In reality, they do not exist singly, Nor are they plural in nature. Why? Because they do not exist."[31]

Reviewing the Purpose of Madhyamaka

We have seen that Svatantrika and Prasangika Madhyamaka both use similar reasonings to bring about the realization of emptiness. In particular, the five great reasonings of Madhyamaka usher forth the realization of the true nature. Emptiness is our meditation. But it is not as if we are trying to make something up or cover up reality with something extra. The true nature of reality is emptiness, and it is this natural state we are connecting with through our meditation. Actually, reconnecting with the true nature is known as "meditation." Meditation is nothing more than simply relaxing and abiding in the nature as it is, without swinging between extreme views.

The roots of this extremism are grasping and clinging, the true hindrances to our realization of emptiness. So the great Madhyamaka masters used the five great reasonings to break down our grasping tendencies and usher us into the absolute nature of emptiness. Grasping and clinging are obstacles to our realization of the true nature because they do not accord with the way things are, with the natural state. They are hindrances because they take us away from the nature. The five Madhyamaka reasonings will smash down and remove our grasping and conceptual fabrications, illuminating the true nature of both subject and object. In his famous *Guide to the Bodhisattva's Way of Life*, Shantideva said, "I do not refute what you see, hear, or think. I refute grasping, which is the cause of suffering." We have completed our discussion of the first four reasoning of Madhyamaka, and will now move on to the fifth.

THE FIFTH GREAT REASONING OF MADHYAMAKA

The fifth great reasoning of Madhyamaka is called the "valid cognition reasoning of dependent origination" or the "great reasoning of dependent arising that eliminates all notions about phenomena." In Tibetan it is called "*Kun la chopa tendrel chenmo tentsig*."[32] *Kun* means "all" and *la* means "to." Once again, *chodpa* means "analyzation," while *tendrel* means "dependent arising" or "dependent origination." *Ten tsig* means "reason" or "valid cognition reasoning." Roughly translated, this is the "great reasoning of dependent origination that analyzes everything."

On the absolute level, phenomena have no true existence based on the fact that they are all completely interrelated. All phenomena are dependent upon each other and connected with one another. Thus, no phenomena truly exist, since results are not brought about by just one cause or condition; actually, each result is dependent upon an entire system of interdependent origination that we do not see. Trillions and trillions of causes and conditions are directly and indirectly interconnected and delicately balanced to produce the objects of our perception. Even the perceiving subject—the very "self" that experiences phenomena—is a combination of many different things.

When we look at an object, it seems as though we are looking at a single thing, but each object is composed of many ingredients. For example, the teachings explain that all outside objects and inner subjects are inseparable from co-origination, or dependent arising. Take the example of a seed: one cause by itself is not enough to produce the result of a seed. There needs to be earth, fire, water, wind, space, and time for the seed to arise. Hence, in order to develop a particular result, or effect, there must be a perfect balance between various causes and conditions.

Additionally, results do not arise immediately. Let us recall the example of a seed. Seeds develop through six or seven different stages, during which they grow roots, sprouts, leaves, flowers, and eventually more seeds. Many stages of development are involved in the production of one simple fruit. In the same way, all results require a very delicate balance between causes and conditions to arise and function. An important part of this balance is the continual involvement of the five principal elements that we just mentioned—earth, fire, water, wind, and space. So when we plant the seed of an apple tree, this tree grows due to the interrelationships between an extraordinary number of causes and conditions, all working in delicate balance. Furthermore, these causes and conditions themselves rely on other causes and conditions, which themselves rely on other causes and conditions, and so on. If even one cause or condition is missing, the seed (i.e. result) will not come. This is something we all know from our own experience.

Look at this building: how many ingredients does it take to construct a single building? Wood is not enough; brick is not enough; hammers are not enough; nails are not enough; planes are not enough; and building permits are not enough. So many things must work together in mutual dependence to produce specific results. Again, if even one of these components is missing, the building will not turn out exactly as we hope. This example demonstrates dependent arising by showing how a "single" objects requires a vast network of interconnectivity to function. No object has any independent, solid existence; phenomena are part of a group effort!

It is important to recognize that even the different ingredients involved in a "single" thing are completely dependent upon many other causes and conditions. That is, each ingredient itself arises due to the complex interactions of many other ingredients. A drop of water, for instance, is composed of many elements. Without one of those elements, the water would cease to be water. This is why phenomenal appearances are referred to as "illusions" or "bubbles."

Dependent arising is not limited to objects; subjects, too, are dependently arisen. In terms of consciousness, many factors are involved in developing a single consciousness, such as eye consciousness. Actually, three principal things are needed to spark eye consciousness. First, we need an object (form) that can be perceived by the eyes. Yet form alone is not enough, since we need an eye organ to perceive the object. Without an eye organ, form will not be seen and eye consciousness will not be sparked. Therefore, the object and the eye organ are necessary, but we also need consciousness based upon an instant of perception, or the intention to look at an object. This analysis of consciousness is taught in Buddhist philosophy.

To summarize, for sight to occur there must be (1) form, (2) an eye organ, and (3) eye consciousness which is based upon an instant of time. This consciousness sparks via the eye organ and makes "contact" with a form, transmitting the perception of form back to the eye in an instant. Also involved in this process is a chain of moments of time associated with the intention to look at an object in the first place. If even a single component of this process is missing, eye consciousness will not occur. Lacking form, nothing will be seen. Similarly, if an eye organ is defective or missing, eye consciousness will not be sparked—one will just experience blankness. Further, if consciousness does not spark at the right time and in the right direction, although objects may be present, they will not be perceived. Lastly, although several people may see the same thing at the same time, some will experience eye consciousness and others will not, because their intention to see was not activated. This process is not mysterious—it is actually how eye consciousness really functions.

From this analysis we can see that three principal ingredients are needed to activate any one of the six consciousnesses, be it eye, ear, nose, tongue, body, or mind consciousness. For instance, at least three things are involved for just one simple idea to arise in our minds. Yet each of these three components—(1) the object of the organ, (2) the organ itself, and (3) the organ consciousness based on an instant of time and activitated by intention—is made up of many different elements. It is the system of dependent origination that allows phenomena to function on the conventional level. This is the nature of reality, which is utterly pervasive: Regardless of whether subject or object is big or small, it functions according to the truth of interdependence. By carefully examining the logic of samsara, we will recognize that samsara itself *is* the system of dependent arising. For this reason, the Blessed One taught the twelve links of dependent origination, which encompass both samsara and nirvana.[33]

Spiritual paths are also based upon the system of dependent origination. Accordingly, meditation and spiritual practice develop stage by stage, founded on the interactions between a practitioners' devotion, joy, and appreciation; no single cause or factor determines spiritual progress, since practice is based upon so many different supports, causes, and conditions. Countless causes and conditions work together to bring about one simple result, so each result is very precious, unique, and special. Everything is in a state of harmony. Good or bad, all things work together, in cooperation. Because phenomena function in this way, they have no substantial, true existence and do not arise due to just one or condition. No single thing has the power to produce a result because results are dependently arisen. Thus all the logic we have explored in our studies of Madhyamaka refutes the substantial, true existence of relative phenomena. Buddha Shakyamuni compared phenomena to "bubbles, mirages, and reflections of the moon in water." He referred to relative truth as "illusory," functioning according to the world of illusion.

In his *Mula-madhyamaka-prajna*, Nagarjuna writes "*Gang chir ten jung ma yin pai, cho ga yodpa ma yin pa, de chir tongpa ma yin pai, cho ga yodpa ma yin no.*"[34] This can be roughly translated as, "Everything arises interdependently, And nothing exists which does not arise in this way; Nothing substantially existent, Exists in the world. These four lines represent some of Nagarjuna's greatest teachings. Nagarjuna's verses establish the truth of dependent origination, or emptiness. Everything in the universe is the union of dependent origination and emptiness. Therefore, phenomena have no core existence since they are all interrelated and connected. All phenomena are in a state of constant change, in which each object is totally dependent upon and supportive of the others. Samsara and nirvana function in this way.

All things occurring within the system of dependent origination do not truly exist; they are like illusions, mirror images, bubbles, dreams, mirages, and reflections of the moon in water. The Awakened One and all the great masters who followed in his footsteps used these examples to awaken us from the hard-headed grasping of duality mind and bring forth a vivid realization of great emptiness in our awareness. But this does not mean we should hold on to the idea of emptiness. All the great practitioners of Tibetan Buddhism meditated upon the profound meaning of dependent origination with equanimity, filled with confidence and joy, thereby achieving high realization.

Absolute Truth and Valid Cognition

What is the nature of absolute truth outside the structure valid cognition? Does absolute truth exist *within* the framework of valid cognition, or is beyond conception altogether? In reality, absolute truth is not encompassed by valid cognition, as it is uncountable and hence totally beyond conception. One who attains high realization of uncountable absolute truth no longer distinguishes between relative and absolute truths; both merge in a single state given that one's own awareness is no longer hindered by grasping and duality. Having freed ourselves from the obscurations associated with duality, we won't have to separate the two truths. After recognizing the nature of uncountable absolute truth, we simply relax in the natural state as it is. This is called "absolute truth not even in keeping with the perspective of valid cognition."

In the ninth chapter of his *Guide to the Bodhisattva's Way of Life*,[35] Shantideva explains that absolute truth is not an object of conception.

Similarly, in the *Madhyamakalankara*, Shantarakshita states, "Since there is no birth, there is no non-birth, either." By deeply investigating and analyzing the nature of existence and nonexistence, we will smash our regimented conceptual fabrications and recognize the absolute nature beyond all duality. Having thus been freed from duality and grasping, we will no longer divide the nature according to our conceptualizations. The true nature is actually indivisible and inexpressible. So, from the ultimate perspective, the distinction between emptiness and form is a mere imputation. This is why the Svatantrikas teach that absolute truth is not included within the scope of valid cognition. Such a realization of emptiness is the same as the Dzogchen view of Trekchod, within which there is nothing to meditate upon and non-meditation is itself the great meditation. In other words, meditation ceases to be a conceptual construction, since mind-made meditation is still based on dualistic fabrication.

Questions and Answers

Question: I don't really trust logic. Can I still practice Madhyamaka?

Answer: Yes. As we said earlier, there are two ways to meditate on emptiness. In the first, we use logic and reason to investigate and analyze the nature, thus bringing forth the realization of emptiness. According to the second approach, we receive direct meditation instructions and practice these instructions with joy, devotion, and trust, bringing forth realization of emptiness is this way. The second approach does not require logic or reason. We are mainly focusing on the first method in this shedra.

But nobody is forcing us to trust or believe in logic; belief is not required. If the logical approach doesn't work for us, that is fine. On the other hand, if we think a particular logical argument is wrong or faulty, it is good to investigate *why* we don't agree with that particular reasoning. In our investigation of the nature, we are supposed to examine the nature very closely, as if testing gold to determine its quality—we are not just talking about the nature or believing in it blindly. We can ask hundreds of questions about the truth of the logic we are exploring. We should ask ourselves, "Is this reasoning correct? Does it make sense?" If we don't agree with a certain point, we can debate it and find common ground.

On the other hand, if we simply don't believe in logic, that's it. There is nothing more to say. However, if we have some kind of disagreement with something we have heard, we can thoroughly investigate that point. It is fine to doubt something. Still, the logical reasonings we have been exploring are renowned, established long ago by great masters. Many people don't really like logic or reasoning; these people can directly investigate the teachings on emptiness by practicing the pith instructions. Actually, the point of logic is to establish the emptiness of the true nature. So, once we discover the deep meaning that logic point to, we can simply practice.

Many great practitioners have chosen to emphasize the second method we just discussed. These great masters didn't really need logic. The entire purpose of Buddhist logic is to uproot harmful misconceptions about the nature. This is why logic was taught and practiced so widely by the great masters of India and Tibet. Yet many great Nyingma and Kagyu masters appeared who didn't really need logic; for such practitioners, logic can be an obstacle that only results in more conceptions. Whether we emphasize the logical approach or the practical approach to arriving at an understanding of emptiness, it is extremely important to engage in meditation practice. We must apply the teachings we have received with confidence, joy, devotion, courage, and commitment to actualize the result.

Question: Earlier you said that Buddha refused to debate relative phenomena. Could you explain this further?

Answer: This generally refers to those times when Buddha Shakyamuni was teaching from the absolute perspective. In such cases, he was not really talking about relative truth. Speaking about absolute truth, he said "no birth, no existence, no cessation," and similar things. Had the Buddha said this to regular beings, they wouldn't have understood. For instance, if a regular being asked him a question about relative truth and he responded with answers such as "no eye, no ear, no nose, and no tongue," they wouldn't have understood. Thus, Buddha Shakyamuni said, "I'm not going to debate with beings or discuss the meaning of absolute truth. I will simply go along with what they say."

The Svatantrika and Prasangika schools follow in the footsteps of the Buddha, since they do not debate relative truth—they only refute the inherent, independent existence of phenomena in order to point out the absolute nature. Madhyamaka practitioners don't talk too much about this or that, arguing the fine points of relative truth. Instead, they simply accept and follow the lead of others.

This teaching method is related with skillful means and compassion. Based upon his infinite compassion, the Blessed One accepted worldly conventions. Yet his compassionate acceptance was not the same as our own; being omniscient, Buddha spontaneously recognized the feelings of other beings and so gave many teaching on bodhichitta. When the time ripened for additional, more profound teachings, the Buddha gave progressively subtler explanations of the Dharma according to the capabilities of beings. Other masters such as Nagarjuna and Asanga later appeared, formally organizing the Buddha's teachings so that they were easy to follow and practice. This happened *after* the time of the Buddha. For example, Nagarjuna and Asanga clarified the meaning of the *Prajnaparamita* teachings on transcendent wisdom. Other great masters compiled sadhanas and different practice methods. Each of these activities is totally connected with the teachings of the Buddha, representing his compassionate skillful means.

Dzogchen and Madhyamaka

The Dzogchen teachings often state that self-awareness is luminous, transparent, lucid, and unimpeded. These words are used to bring forth a clear picture of the true nature as it is. The nature is pure from the beginning, so nothing needs to be added or subtracted, and everything is perceived within a state of fullness and wakefulness. In the *Prajnaparamita Sutras*, the Buddha taught that the true nature neither increases nor decreases; there is nothing to gain and nothing to lose. Therefore, Dzogchen explains that everything is self-liberated when we simply relax in awareness of the nature. There is no need to forcefully liberate conceptions, constructions, or illusions. In fact, from the ultimate perspective of uncountable absolute truth, all dichotomies of liberating and not liberating, emptiness and form are mental fabrications. They are conceptual boundaries that mind creates for itself, based on duality. The great master Chandrakirti explains in the *Madhyamakavatara* that "sentient beings are bound by conceptions, whereas Buddhas are not bound by any conceptions whatsoever. By relaxing in the absolute state, you will release the knots and boundaries (that obscure the nature)."

Practicing Madhyamaka is the same as practicing Dzogchen. In both cases we should always begin with strong devotion, joy, appreciation, and bodhichitta. The prayers we recite are our expressions of love, compassion, joy, and devotion in the form of words that echo the beautiful qualities of mind. These special words invoke our hidden qualities and encourage them to flourish. As the Vajrayana teachings often state, practicing in this way will cleanse the dullness of our channels, winds, nervous systems, and minds, bringing forth a dense freshness.

Along with these beautiful thoughts and prayers, we are going to unite the two truths together in the Madhyamaka state. As we have seen throughout our studies, the two truths are inherently inseparable, so there is no need to make the distinction between absolute and relative during practice. When you meditate, just relax. Let go of thoughts such as, "I'll only do this" or "I don't like that." Instead, rest your mind in the Dzogchen state of great emptiness. During post-meditation, perform as many good deeds as possible—related with the six paramitas—according to your capabilities.[36] Together, meditation and post-meditation activity are known as the "accumulation of the two merits of (1) wisdom and (2) meritorious activity," united without discrimination. Here we are not judging this as "good" and that as "bad."

The Mahayana teachings frequently speak of ground, path, and fruition: the ground is a union because the two truths are inseparable; the path is a union because the two accumulations of wisdom and merit are always practiced together; finally, based upon this practice, fruition is a union of the two kayas (dharmakaya and rupakaya). This is known as full achievement, or realization. Teachings on the two truths are found not only in Madhyamaka, but in all schools of Buddhism. This is true for the Vaibashika school all the way up to Ati Yoga, or Dzogchen. Every Buddhist school teaches the two truths.

Conclusion

We have now concluded our brief teachings on Svatantrika Madhyamaka, one of the most renowned schools of Mahayana Buddhism. Again, there is little difference between Svatantrika and Prasangika Madhyamaka; both schools belong to the Mahayana tradition and are extremely special, establishing the very ground of Dzogchen and Mahamudra teachings. But Madhyamaka is not only a philosophical teaching—it is a practice. When you have time, it is good to meditate on the meaning of great emptiness according to the great reasonings of Madhyamaka and their analyses. Whether one practices Dzogchen, Mahamudra, or another Buddhist practice, the nature is the same. Every road leads to the same goal, so we should relax and meditate on this beautiful nature. The great Longchenpa taught that each practice session can be divided in three ways: (1) the beginning includes cultivating bodhichitta and devotion; (2) the middle includes engaging in the main practice, such as Madhyamaka, free from grasping or clinging; and (3) the end includes reciting aspiration and dedication prayers on behalf of all sentient beings.

Thank you everyone for coming here to participate in this wonderful shedra. Once again, it has truly been one of the most beautiful, special, and memorable occasions of our lives, up here on our beautiful retreat land of Padma Samye Ling, the Inconceivable Lotus Land. We are very grateful and happy that the Dharma continues to flourish, and we pray that we can continue to engage in these activities for many, many aeons in the future. May the Dharma continually spark throughout this world and the rest of the universe. Just as space explorers go farther and farther into the depths of the universe, we too have the special challenge of exploring the vastness of Dharma, which is as limitless as space. Hopefully the glorious message of the teachings will extend far into the future, reaching and benefitting all beings who come in contact with it. We all pray for this.

We have all enjoyed the excellent opportunity to discuss the Svatantrika Madhyamaka teachings during this year's shedra. These particular teachings come from the great master Shantarakshita, who came to Tibet in the 8th century. The wisdom of the great beings whose teachings we have explored is far beyond the realms of conception. And although our wisdom is not exactly equal to that of the ancient masters, we have presented the teachings to the best of our abilities. The masters we have discussed truly explored the nature, achieving a realization that few have reached.

Shantarakshita, Vairochana, Chokro Lui Gyaltsen, Kawa Paltsek, Shang Yeshe De and others brought these teachings to Tibet about 1,200 years ago. Along with the twenty-five disciples of Guru Padmasambhava, they were truly great explorers of reality. But these teachers did not explore the exterior world; rather, they explored the inner realms, bringing forth unsurpassed realization and achievement within themselves. Waves of knowledge and wisdom continually echoed throughout the valleys, land, and countryside of Tibet. As a result, century after century, many great beings appeared from all the different schools of Tibetan Buddhism, one after another. These beings honored and upheld the Madhyamaka teachings of Shantarakshita that we have been discussing. Even though we didn't have time to discuss everything in depth, we have taught according to the Madhyamaka tradition of Longchenpa, Shantarakshita, and Mipham Rinpoche. This was our intention.

Yet it is not as though we have merely been trying to learn something new during this shedra. We have also been glorifying the memory of all the remarkable masters who continually upheld and spread these teachings for the benefit of all beings. They genuinely embodied love, compassion, and wisdom. It is said that Trisong Deutsen, along with the help of other Tibetan masters, created twelve big institutes and twelve big retreat centers—twenty-four in all—to maintain and study the profound teachings of the Dharma. The famous masters and scholars of the eleventh and twelfth centuries studied the precious Svatantrika Madhyamaka teachings according to the tradition of the great Shantarakshita, and his teaching lineage has been upheld and glorified until the present.

We have all had the special opportunity to study here at the beautiful Padma Samye Ling, which were able to build through your kindness, compassion, and love. Now we are really trying to activitate the monastery according to our capabilities. We are so grateful that all of us have had the opportunity to come here together, and we wish to thank everyone who has participated in and helped organize this beautiful shedra. We wish you all good health, joy, peace, and happiness—and a lot of realization. Hopefully we will see you again soon here or some other place! Thank you.

Dedication

May the victory banner of the fearless teachings of
the ancient tradition be raised.
May the victorious drum of the teaching and practice of Dharma
resound in the ten directions.
May the lion's roar of reasoning pervade the three places.
May the light of unequalled virtues increase.

May all the temples and monasteries,
All the readings and recitations of the Dharma flourish.
May the sangha always be in harmony,
And may their aspirations be achieved.

At this very moment for the peoples and nations of the earth,
May not even the names disease, famine, war,
and suffering be heard.
But rather may pure conduct, merit, wealth, and
prosperity increase,
And may supreme good fortune and well being always arise.

About the Authors

Khenchen Palden Sherab Rinpoche

Venerable Khenchen Palden Sherab Rinpoche is a renowned scholar and meditation master of Nyingma, the Ancient School of Tibetan Buddhism.

He was born on May 10, 1942 in the Dhoshul region of Kham, Eastern Tibet, near the sacred mountain Jowo Zegyal. On the morning of his birth a small snow fell with the flakes in the shape of lotus petals. Among his ancestors were many great scholars, practitioners, and treasure revealers.

His family was semi-nomadic, living in the village during the winter and moving with the herds to high mountain pastures where they lived in yak hair tents during the summers. The monastery for the Dhoshul region is called Gochen and his father's family had the hereditary responsibility for administration of the business affairs of the monastery. His grandfather had been both administrator and chantmaster in charge of the ritual ceremonies.

He started his education at the age of four at Gochen monastery, which was founded by Tsasum Lingpa. At the age of twelve he entered Riwoche monastery and completed his studies just before the Chinese invasion of Tibet reached that area. His root teacher was the illustrious Khenpo Tenzin Dragpa (Katog Khenpo Akshu).

In 1960, Rinpoche and his family were forced into exile, escaping to India. Eventually in 1967 he was appointed head of the Nyingmapa department of the Central Institute of Higher Tibetan Studies in Sarnath. He held this position for seventeen years, as an abbot, dedicating all his time and energy to ensure the survival and spread of the Buddhist teachings.

Rinpoche moved to the United States in 1984 to work closely with H.H. Dudjom Rinpoche, the supreme head of the Nyingmapa lineage. In 1985, Venerable Khenchen Palden Sherab Rinpoche and his brother Venerable Khenpo Tsewang Dongyal Rinpoche founded the Dharma Samudra Publishing Company. In 1988, they founded the Padmasambhava Buddhist Center, which has centers throughout the United States, as well as in Puerto Rico, Russia and India. The primary center is Padma Samye Ling, located in Delaware County, New York. Padmasambhava Buddhist Center also includes a traditional Tibetan Buddhist monastery and nunnery at the holy site of Deer Park in Sarnath, India.

Rinpoche travels extensively within the United States and throughout the world, giving teachings and empowerments at numerous retreats and seminars, in addition to establishing meditation centers.

His three volumes of collected works in Tibetan include:

Opening the Eyes of Wisdom, a commentary on Sangye Yeshe's *Lamp of the Eye of Contemplation*;

Waves of the Ocean of Devotion, a biography-praise to Nubchen Sangye Yeshe, and *Vajra Rosary*, biographies of his main incarnations;

The Mirror of Mindfulness, an explanation of the six bardos;

Advice from the Ancestral Vidyadhara, a commentary on Padmasambhava's *Stages of the Path, Heap of Jewels*;

Blazing Clouds of Wisdom and Compassion, a commentary on the hundred-syllable mantra of Vajrasattva;

The Ornament of Vairochana's Intention, a commentary on the *Heart Sutra*;

Opening the Door of Blessings, a biography of Machig Labdron;

Lotus Necklace of Devotion, a biography of Khenchen Tenzin Dragpa;

The Essence of Diamond Clear Light, an outline and structural analysis of *The Aspiration Prayer of Samantabhadra*;

The Lamp of Blazing Sun and Moon, a commentary on Mipham's *Wisdom Sword*;
The Ornament of Stars at Dawn, an outline and structural analysis of Vasubandhu's *Twenty Verses*;
Pleasure Lake of Nagarjuna's Intention, general summary of Madhyamaka;
Supreme Clear Mirror, an introduction to Buddhist logic;
White Lotus, an explanation of prayers to Guru Rinpoche;
Smiling Red Lotus, short commentary on the prayer to Yeshe Tsogyal;
Clouds of Blessings; an explanation of prayers to Terchen Tsasum Lingpa; and other learned works, poems, prayers and sadhanas.

Khenpo Tsewang Dongyal Rinpoche

Venerable Khenpo Tsewang Dongyal Rinpoche was born in the Dhoshul region of Kham in eastern Tibet on June 10, 1950. On that summer day in the family tent, Rinpoche's birth caused his mother no pain. The next day, his mother Pema Lhadze moved the bed where she had given birth. Beneath it she found growing a beautiful and fragrant flower which she plucked and offered to Chenrezig on the family altar.

Soon after his birth three head lamas from Jadchag monastery came to his home and recognized him as the reincarnation of Khenpo Sherab Khyentse. Khenpo Sherab Khyentse, who had been the former head abbot lama at Gochen monastery, was a renowned scholar and practitioner who spent much of his life in retreat.

Rinpoche's first Dharma teacher was his father, Lama Chimed Namgyal Rinpoche. Beginning his schooling at the age of five, he entered Gochen monastery. His studies were interrupted by the Chinese invasion and his family's escape to India. In India his father and brother continued his education until he entered the Nyingmapa Monastic School of northern India, where he studied until 1967. He then entered the Central Institute of Higher Tibetan Studies, which was then a part of Sanskrit University in Varanasi, where he received his B.A. degree in 1975. He also attended Nyingmapa University in West Bengal, where he received another B.A. and an M.A. in 1977.

In 1978, Rinpoche was enthroned as the abbot of the Wish-fulfilling Nyingmapa Institute in Boudanath, Nepal by H.H. Dudjom Rinpoche, and later became the abbot of the Department of Dharma Studies, where he taught poetry, grammar, philosophy and psychology. In 1981, H.H. Dudjom Rinpoche appointed Rinpoche as the abbot of the Dorje

Nyingpo center in Paris, France. In 1982 he was asked to work with H.H. Dudjom Rinpoche at the Yeshe Nyingpo center in New York. During the 1980's, until H.H. Dudjom Rinpoche's mahaparinirvana in 1987, Rinpoche continued working closely with H.H. Dudjom Rinpoche, often traveling with him as his translator and attendant.

In 1988, Rinpoche and his brother founded the Padmasambhava Buddhist Center. Since that time he has served as a spiritual director at the various Padmasambhava centers throughout the world. He maintains an active traveling and teaching schedule with his brother Khenchen Palden Sherab Rinpoche.

Khenpo Tsewang Rinpoche has authored two books of poetry on the life of Guru Rinpoche, including *Praise to the Lotus Born: A Verse Garland of Waves of Devotion*, and a unique two-volume cultural and religious history of Tibet entitled *The Six Sublime Pillars of the Nyingma School*, which details the historical bases of the Dharma in Tibet from the sixth through ninth centuries. At present, this is one of the only books yet written that conveys the dharma activities of this historical period in such depth. Khenpo Rinpoche has also co-authored a number of books in English on Dharma subjects with his brother Khenchen Palden Sherab Rinpoche, including *Ceaseless Echoes of the Great Silence: A Commentary on the Heart Sutra*; *Prajnaparamita: The Six Perfections*; *Door to Inconceivable Wisdom and Compassion*; *Lion's Gaze: A Commentary on the Tsig Sum Nedek*; and *Opening Our Primordial Nature*.

Other Publications by the Authors

Ceaseless Echoes of the Great Silence:
A Commentary on the Heart Sutra

Prajnaparamita: The Six Perfections

Light of the Three Jewels

Lion's Gaze: A Commentary on the Tsig Sum Nedek

Door to Inconceivable Wisdom and Compassion

Praise to the Lotus Born: A Verse Garland of Waves of Devotion

The Smile of Sun and Moon

Opening to Our Primordial Nature

Opening the Clear Vision of the Vaibhashika and Sautrantika Schools

Opening the Clear Vision of the Mind Only School

Opening the Wisdom Door of the Rangtong and Shentong Views:
A Brief Explanation of the One Taste of the Second
and Third Turnings of the Wheel of Dharma

More information about these and other works by
the Venerable Khenpo Rinpoches can be found online at:
www.padmasambhava.org/chiso.

EndNotes

[1] Bracketed text indicates the Wylie transliteration of the Tibetan term.

[2] The two merits refer to (1) the accumulation merit and (2) the wisdom merit.

[3] Mipham Jamyang Namgyal Gyatso, or Mipham Rinpoche, was a renowned Nyingma scholar and master who lived from 1845-1912. He was a student of Jamyang Khyentse Wangpo (his root guru), Jamgön Kongtrul the Great, and Patrul Rinpoche. His primary disciple was Shechen Gyaltsab Pema Namgyal, who later became the root guru of Dilgo Khyentse Rinpoche. Even though Mipham Rinpoche had attained the very highest realization, he was a simple and humble wandering-hermitage monk. Considered to be an emanation of Manjushri and Nubchen Sangye Yeshe, Mipham's printed works fill thirty-two volumes. He wrote diversely, from his own direct knowledge, on topics from all ten sciences. These became the textbooks used in all the Nyingma monastic institutions.

[4] The three yana classification refers to the Hinayana, Mahayana, and Vajrayana, respectively. In contrast, the Nyingma school divides the teachings into nine yanas: the three Sutrayanas of the Shravakas, Pratyekabuddhas, and Bodhisattvas; the three Outer Tantras of Kriyatantra, Upatantra (or Charyatantra), and Yogatantra; and the three Inner Tantras of Mahayoga, Anuyoga, and Atiyoga, or Dzogchen—the pinnacle of all vehicles.

[5] In the Dzogchen context, "view" refers to a correct philosophical orientation and understanding of the true nature of reality, upon which we base our practice of meditation.

[6] The Wylie transliteration: "*dBu ma rtsa ba'i tshig le'ur byas pa shes rab ces bya ba.*"

[7] The Wylie transliteration: "*dBu ma'i rtsa ba'i 'grel pa shes rab sgron ma*"; in Skt. *Tarkajvala* or *Prajna-pradipa-mula-madhyamaka-vrtti*]

[8] The full version of the Sanskrit title: *Madhyamaka-hrdaya-karika*. The Wylie transliteration: "*dBu ma'i snying po'i tshig le'ur byas pa*."

[9] Shantarakshita is referred to by many names, including "Khenchen Bodhisattva," "Abbot Shantarakshita," "The Great Preceptor," and "Shiwatso" (literally, "Protector of Peace") among others.

[10] The Tibetan titles are "*dBu ma rgyan*" and "*dBu ma rgyan gyi 'grel pa*," respectively.

[11] The first six consciousnesses are associated with the six senses: sight, sound, smell, taste, touch, and mind. The seventh consciousness is *klesha* mind, related with the sense of "I," "me," and "mine," along with pride and arrogance. The eighth consciousness is the *alaya*, or the "subconscious storehouse" upon which habitual imprints of perception and karma, for example, are stored.

[12] The Sanskrit word *karma* literally means "action," with the implied meaning of action performed with volition or intention.

[13] According to the Padmakara Translation Group, the terms Prasangika and Svatantrika "are Sanskrit renditions, contrived by Western scholars, of two Tibetan terms (*rang gyud pa* and *thal 'gyur pa* respectively). It is important to realize that the Svatantrika-Prasangika distinction, as such, is the invention of Tibetan scholarship, created as a convenient method for cataloging the different viewpoints evident in Madhyamika authors subsequent to Chandrakirti's critique of Bhavaviveka. There is no evidence that these two terms were ever used by the ancient Indian Madhyamikas to refer either to themselves or their opponents." From *Introduction to the Middle Way: Chandrakirti's Madhyamakavatara With Commentary By Jamgön Mipham*, translated by Padmakara Translation Group. Boston: Shambhala, 2002. p.35.)

[14] This refers to the disciples of Guru Padmasambhava, Vimalamitra, and Shantarakshita who dwelled in the Yerpa region, northeast of Lhasa.

[15] Around the end of the 9th and beginning of the 10th centuries, the master

Dorje Denpa performed a big ganachakra ceremony in Bodhgaya, inviting many of the greatest Indian masters of the time to participate.

[16] The Wylie transliteration: "*dBu ma rgran gyi rnam bshad 'jam dbyangs bla ma dgyes pa'i zhal lung*."

[17] Asanga spent many years in solitary retreat practicing on Maitreya, but achieved no signs of accomplishment. After becoming discouraged several times and nearly giving up, Asanga eventually met the tenth-bhumi bodhisattva and regent of Buddha Shakyamuni face-to-face. Maitreya then took Asanga to his pureland, Tushita Heaven, where he gave him extensive teachings on the Mahayana, including the *Five Treatises of Maitreya*. The *Uttaratantra*, or *Ratna-gotra-vibhaga*, is one such treatise.

[18] Contrasting accurate relative truth, mistaken relative truth refers to completely misperceiving things: Not only do we not experience the pure perception of buddhas and bodhisattvas, but we perceive phenomena incorrectly due to some physical defect of the senses, or something similar. For instance, we may see the color white as yellow due to jaundice, or perhaps we see double images due to cataracts. These perceptions are mistaken from both the relative and absolute perspectives.

[19] Visualizing the deities in union is generally related with the practice of the Inner Tantras.

[20] There are eight traditional analogies used to describe the illusory nature of phenomena: (1) dream; (2) illusion; (3) optical illusion; (4) mirage; (5) reflection of the moon in water; (6) echo; (7) a castle in the sky (city of gandharvas); and (8) an emanation or phantom.

[21] Ringu Tulku offers a nice general overview of the five reasonings of Madhyamaka: "Madhyamaka has five great reasonings: the first four are connected with refuting misunderstandings, and the fifth is connected with establishing correct understanding. In terms of what is refuted, first, causes are analyzed and invalidated through the reasoning called "the diamond

fragments." Second, results are analyzed and invalidated through the reasoning called "the production and cessation of existence and nonexistence." Third, causes and results are analyzed together and invalidated through the reasoning called "the production and cessation of the four alternatives." Fourth, the nature itself is analyzed and invalidated through the reasoning called "free of one and many," and fifth, emptiness is established by analyzing appearances through the reasoning of interdependence." From *The Ri-me Philosophy of Jamgön Kongtrul the Great*, pp. 199-200.

[22] The Wylie transliteration: "*rGyu la dpyod pa rdo rje gzegs ma'i gtan tshigs.*"

[23] Rongzompa, or Rongzom Pandita Chokyi Sangpo (1012-1088) is regarded as one of the greatest scholars in Nyingma history, along with Longchenpa.

[24] The Wylie transliteration: "*Dras bu la dpyod pa yod med skye 'gog gi gtan tshigs.*"

[25] The Wylie transliteration: "*bDag las ma yin gzhan las min, gnyis las ma yin rgyu med min, gnos po gang dag gang na yang, skye ba nam yang yod ma yin.*" Khenpo Tsültrim Gyamtso translates this verse in his *Sun of Wisdom*: "Not from self, not from other, Not from both, nor without cause: Things do not arise At any place, at any time."

[26] The Wylie transliteration: "*Yod pa skye ba rigs min te, med pa'ng nam ka'i me tog bzhin, de ltar yod dang med pa la, mkas pa nam yang mi bzhed do.*" This can be roughly translated as, "Birth of something that exists is illogical. Birth of something that doesn't exist is like a flower in the sky. The same is true of something that is said to both exist and not exist. The wise do not cling to any views."

[27] The Wylie transliteration: "*rGyu 'bras gnyis ka la dpyod pa mu bzhi'i skye 'gog gi gtan tshigs.*"

[28] This reasoning is shared by all Madhyamaka schools.

[29] The full Wylie transliteration of Jnanagarbha's quote: "*dBu ma bden gnyis las,*

Du mas gcig gi dngos mi byed, Du mas du ma byed ma yin, gCig gis du ma'i dngos mi byed, gCig gis gcig byed pa yang min, Zhes so."

[30] The Wylie transliteration: "*Ngo bo la dpyod pa gcig du ma brel gyi gtan tshigs.*"

[31] The Wylie transliteration: "*bDag dang gzhan smras dngos 'di dag, yang dag du na gcig pa dang, du ma'i rang bzhin bral ba'i phyir, rang bzhin med de gzugs brnyan bzhin.*" This can be translated into English as follows: "All the things that are spoken of by both Buddhist and Non-Buddhist schools do not have any inherent existence, because they are devoid of singularity and plurality."

[32] The Wylie transliteration: "*Kun la dpyod pa rten 'brel chen mo'i gtan tshigs.*"

[33] The twelve links of dependent origination are: (1) ignorance, (2) habitual tendencies, (3) consciousness, (4) name and form, (5) the six activity fields of the eye, ear, nose, tongue, body, and mind, (6) contact, (7) sensation, (8) craving, (9) clinging, (10) becoming, (11) birth, (12) old age and death.

[34] The Wylie transliteration: "*Gang phyir rten 'byung ma yin pa'i, chos 'ga' yod pa ma yin pa, de phyir stong pa ma yin pa'i, chos 'ga' yod pa ma yin no.*" Negatively stated, this can be translated as, "Because something which has not dependently arisen, Does not exist in the world, Something which is not empty (of inherent existence), Does not exist in the world."

[35] The ninth chapter of this famous work is related with transcendent wisdom, or *prajna*.

[36] The "six paramitas," or transcendental perfections, are: (1) generosity, (2) moral discipline, (3) patience, (4) diligence, (5) concentration, and (6) wisdom.

Printed in the United States
86184LV00004B/103-192/A

9 780965 933964